D0149420

Praise for
I'll Bring the Chocolate

"Karen Porter's *I'll Bring the Chocolate* is a basketful of goodies: humor, insight, prayer, recipes, great quotations, and inspiration to encourage women in their faith and friendships."

—KAREN O'CONNOR, speaker and author of *Gettin' Old Ain't For Wimps* and *The Beauty of Aging*

"Every woman can and will discover a sweet spot of relational satisfaction in the pages of *I'll Bring the Chocolate*. Karen Porter nourishes the friendship soul with great writing and the 'Give me more chocolate!' soul with drop-dead delicious recipes."

—JULIE BARNHILL, International Speaker and author of bestselling *She's Gonna Blow!*

"What's better than a box of chocolates? A pan of brownies? A chocolate milkshake? Eating them while savoring *I'll Bring the Chocolate*! Karen Porter has given new meaning to the word 'YUM'!"

—EVA MARIE EVERSON, author of *Oasis, A Spa for Body & Soul*

"Karen Porter understands that God's love, like the richest chocolate, is an absolute daily necessity in life. Use with abandon."

—VIRELLE KIDDER, conference speaker and author of *Meet Me at the Well: Take a Month to Water Your Soul*

"Karen Porter has given us a gourmet recipe for biblically-based friendships. With a delightful combination of personal authenticity, laugh-out-loud humor, prized family recipes, and enduring truth, this book will be one of your new favorites."

—CAROL KENT, speaker and author of *A New Kind of Normal*

"Karen Porter provides a marvelous assortment of wit, wisdom, and delightful recipes. If you yearn for authentic friendships in the midst of today's hectic pace, then you will savor *I'll Bring the Chocolate*."

—GEORGIA SHAFFER, licensed psychologist, life coach, and author of *A Gift of Mourning Glories*

"Let Karen Porter entice you away from the lists and the laundry, the carpooling and the computer to savor the sweetness of spiritual friendships—the shared faith, the encouragement, and the comforting loyalty."

—LAEL ARRINGTON, author of *Worldproofing Your Kids* and cohost of *The Things That Matter Most* talk radio

"Karen Porter will treat you to a helping of her friendship and faith as well as mouthwatering recipes and chocolate descriptions. You'll enjoy every bite."

—LINDA EVANS SHEPHERD, speaker and coauthor of *The Potluck Club*

I'll Bring the
Chocolate

I'll Bring the Chocolate

Satisfying a Woman's Craving for Friendship and Faith

Karen Porter

MULTNOMAH
BOOKS

I'LL BRING THE CHOCOLATE
PUBLISHED BY MULTNOMAH BOOKS
12265 Oracle Boulevard, Suite 200
Colorado Springs, Colorado 80921
A division of Random House Inc.

All Scripture quotations, unless otherwise indicated, are taken from the Holy Bible, New International Version®. NIV®. Copyright © 1973, 1978, 1984 by International Bible Society. Used by permission of Zondervan Publishing House. All rights reserved. Scripture quotations marked (TLB) are taken from The Living Bible, copyright © 1971. Used by permission of Tyndale House Publishers Inc., Wheaton, Illinois 60189. All rights reserved. Scripture quotations marked (MSG) are taken from The Message by Eugene H. Peterson. Copyright © 1993, 1994, 1995, 1996, 2000, 2001, 2002. Used by permission of NavPress Publishing Group. All rights reserved. Scripture quotations marked (NASB) are taken from the New American Standard Bible®. © Copyright The Lockman Foundation 1960, 1962, 1963, 1968, 1971, 1972, 1973, 1975, 1977. Used by permission. (www.Lockman.org). Scripture quotations marked (KJV) are taken from the King James Version. Scripture quotations marked (NCV) are taken from the New Century Version®. Copyright © 1987, 1988, 1991 by Thomas Nelson Inc. Used by permission. All rights reserved. Scripture quotations marked (NTL) are taken from the Holy Bible, New Living Translation, copyright © 1996. Used by permission of Tyndale House Publishers Inc., Wheaton, Illinois 60189. All rights reserved.

Recipes created by Cherry McGregor, owner of Elegant Events, Houston, Texas.

Names were changed in the stories about Glen, Elizabeth, Glenda, William, Leeann, Eddie, Vickie, and Annie.

ISBN 978-1-59052-957-7

Library of Congress Cataloging-in-Publication Data
Porter, Karen.
  I'll bring the chocolate / Karen Porter.—1st ed.
      p. cm.
  Includes bibliographical references.
  ISBN 978-1-59052-957-7
1. Christian women—Religious life. 2. Female friendship—Religious
aspects—Christianity. I. Title.
BV4527.P66 2007
248.8'43—dc22

                              2007017516

Printed in the United States of America
2007—First Edition

10 9 8 7 6 5 4 3 2 1

To George.
Best friend,
lifelong love,
better than chocolate ice cream
with chocolate topping with chocolate sprinkles.

Contents

Acknowledgments

$\mathcal{T}$hank you:

Cherry McGregor, daughter and friend, for your love for me and for your gourmet talents. I would be nothing without your friendship, your enthusiasm. I am amazed with what you've done with your life and the remarkable godly woman you have become.

Kathryn Porter, daughter and friend, for your discernment and suggestions. Your rich, clever insights amaze me. Your willingness to follow Jesus wherever He takes you is an inspiration and a motivation to me every day. I am so happy to call you friend, and I love growing closer to you.

Mom, my forever friend. Thanks for your unconditional love for all these years. You've modeled these principles and loved Jesus right before my eyes.

Brett and Craig. You boys make a mama proud. Brett, your spiritual depth astounds me and inspires me to fully follow Jesus in new and fresh ways. Craig, your spiritual enthusiasm spurs me on to a deeper and more vigorous faith. Thank you, guys, for loving me, for praying for me, and for devoting yourselves to fatherhood of the world's most beautiful grandbabies.

My writing club girls—encourager Lael Arrington, creative Kathy Blossom, godly Rooney Williams, eagle eye Katie McDivitt, and fun-loving Janie Carver. How you've blessed me with your love and helpfulness, not to mention suggestions, editing, and consistent urging that this book point to Jesus.

Janet Grant, agent *extraordinaire*. You are the best! Your insight and creativity reign. You are the queen of catchy titles. Thank you for everything.

Georgia Shaffer, friend, encourager, motivator. Thanks for your deep study of this manuscript and your wisdom.

Nancy Bauer, my chocolate-truffle friend. How empty my life would be without you.

Terry Larson. How I love your friendship, your phone calls, and your "I love yous!"

My girlfriends at AWSA, for your friendship and gentle pushing: Lael Arrington, Carole Lewis, Linda Shepherd, Marita Littauer, Virelle Kidder, and Betty Voshage. It matters that you believe in me.

Anita Renfroe, for teaching me the joy and laughter of friendship and for giving of yourself so freely. Girl, you are the best.

Edith Farley. Friendship like ours flows from the heart. Adversity cannot freeze the flow. The enemy found one tiny kink in our armor, but we beat him away, didn't we? Love ya, friend.

Brian Thomasson and Steffany Woolsey, editors at Multnomah. Brian, thank you for your careful attention to me and this project. Steffany, thank you for your exceptional work on this manuscript and for teaching me along the way. Your work has transformed my words. I am deeply grateful for your expertise and even more thankful for your encouragement.

Thank you to all the preachers, teachers, speakers, and authors who have faithfully put God's truths before me over the years. I am so grateful to you for my spiritual growth. For many years I took extensive notes and didn't record who said or wrote what. Much of this information has infiltrated my brain and become such a part of me that it seems like my thoughts. So if you see something in this book that originated with you, please let me know and I'll give you all the credit. Please know that my use of it without your name is a mistake of the head, not the heart.

Jesus, best friend and my Lord. You are the ultimate life-saver, faith giver, encourager, and loyal forgiver who brings joy and freedom.

Foreword

I have many reasons to give thanks. Many. And not the least of them is that I am several years past forty and no longer give a hoot about what anyone else thinks of me (if they ever *do* think of me).

I get to travel around the country helping women remember that laughter is good medicine and that we are in on the divine comedy. (You *are* aware that God has a great sense of humor, right? He made noses, hyenas, and babies' giggles. Need I elaborate?)

I have a great husband, three stellar kids, and a killer recipe for chocolate gravy. That's right, I said chocolate gravy. Let me tell you, only a Southern woman with limited ingredients and a monster case of PMS could have dreamed that one up. But if you ever come to my house, even on extremely short notice, I will whip you up a batch in under twelve minutes and we can soon be drowning something or other in a pool of gastronomic bliss.

Ah, the power of chocolate. It's absolutely magical for soothing the soul and satisfying the taste buds. And for that, I am one grateful chick. I am happy to report that medical science is confirming what women have known for centuries: Chocolate is actually good for us. (As if we needed a reason to imbibe!) Scientists confirm that the strong stuff (over 65 percent cocoa content) has antioxidants, vasodilators, antidepressants, and the Lord Himself only knows what else. We girls just know we *need* it. Not just want it, not just enjoy it—chocolate qualifies as a bona fide female necessity! It ranks right up there with water and air. And although it is not recognized as such by the United States Department of Agriculture, every woman knows chocolate is its own food group.

Whenever I am invited to perform at a ladies' night out, I'm always excited when the event planner tells me they will be serving a chocolate buffet, complete with chocolate fountains, following my presentation. This basically means that the pressure is off me. I could stand up there and read the phone book in a monotone and still be assured the women won't care; the only thing they're hearing is the loop in their head that says, "In just a few minutes I am going to be given access to unlimited chocolate. Woo-hoo!"

I am woman; therefore, I am thankful for chocolate by virtue of gender. But women are also aware of deep-seated needs for things besides chocolate. We know we need a good, supportive bra, as well as a sense of purpose and destiny for our lives. (Not necessarily in that order, but if you have an ill-fitting brassiere, you are going to be crabby and less-than-optimal in the pursuit of your God-given destiny.)

And we crave true, godly friendships. Not friendships that sit on the surface like oil in a glass of water, but the kind that mixes well. The kind of friendship that takes time to develop: mutual admiration, trust, genuine respect, honesty, accountability, generosity, freedom, understanding, history, hospitality, and lots and lots of unconditional love.

You know as well as I do that these types of friendships don't come along every day. It takes finding the right person and *being the right person* for such friendships to flourish. Besides, after a certain point you simply *must* remain friends because, like the Mafia, you just plain know too much.

This is where my second point of gratitude develops—for my friend Karen Porter. She "gets it"—the whole female friendship thing. She understands the dynamics of "girlfriend-ship" because these principles she lays before you are not hypotheses or untested formulas that she concocted out of thin air. These foundational precepts regarding the potential for rich relationships between girlfriends are based on the Handbook for Life, the Bible, and are borne out by the experiences in Karen's own life.

It has been my privilege to count Karen Porter as a friend, and I know that before you finish reading this book, you'll feel like she is your friend too. She speaks from the heart, and she also listens with her heart. True to her Texas roots, she shoots straight from the hip when giving you the skinny. And true to her southern sensibilities, she lays it all out with a generous helping of fun.

Inside the pages of this book you will find practical principles, good girlfriend guidance, mouthwatering recipes, and sustenance for your soul. Pretty great for less than the price of a box of chocolates, wouldn't you say? So settle in, and let Karen take you through a chocolate-covered wonderland of women's friendship.

I echo the psalmist David, who told us to "taste and see that the LORD is good." Though I have no theological support for it, I wholeheartedly believe that when he wrote those words, he must have been thinking of chocolate.

—*Anita Renfroe*
Comedian, author, chocolate lover

Introduction

*F*riends and chocolate—what a great combination. Friends are a woman's greatest treasures, and chocolate is one of the premium foods in existence. As *Houston Business Journal* president Don Miller once wrote, "No matter how bad a cook you are, you can't really screw up a chocolate dish. An unsuccessful fudge can still be used as an excellent ice cream topping; unsuccessful brownies can be explained away as chocolate pudding; and an unsuccessful chocolate soufflé makes an attractive beret."[1]

I once spoke to a Christian sorority at a large university. There were thousands of young, bright, beautiful nineteen- to twenty-two-year-olds gathered at the woodsy campground, all of them decked out in sweatshirts with the words *Soul Sister* silkscreened on the front. We enjoyed a snowy weekend filled with wonderful worship and teaching sessions. They were the most responsive audience I've ever addressed.

But on our last afternoon I spoke about the need for friendship, using the first seeds of material in this book. To my dismay, my words fell flat on their ears and hearts.

Their response puzzled me. I have spoken on friendship to women's groups all over the country, and before this incident the response was, without exception, wonderful. In fact, in my experience, women *love* being encouraged in their friendships. They bond over the topic. Healing from hurt and disappointment takes place. Women's ministries are transformed.

So why did this same message fail to inspire and motivate the college girls? The answer finally dawned on me. Friendship is life to a coed. As soon as a young woman moves into a dorm or apartment, she begins to weave friendships. Every class, study session, activity, ball game, club, and conversation centers on friends.

But when that same girl gets married or moves into single life building a career, she focuses on home, office, family, and a hundred other stresses. And she loses contact with her friends. These girls couldn't relate to the desire for strong female relationships because they hadn't yet experienced the divide that comes with all the responsibilities of being an adult. They were still living the friendship dream! But adult women devour the chance to develop friendships and bond with other women.

Women often feel lonely and isolated. Whether they work in an office or as a full-time stay-at-home mom, they need and crave friendships.

Mitsugi Saotome, chief instructor of aikido martial arts, teaches his students to be strong and self-sufficient through discipline and self-control. While we might disagree with some of his spiritual views, he understands that if we try to live without friends, life is vague. Mitsugi says, "If you were all alone in the universe with no one to talk to, no one with whom to share the beauty of the stars, to laugh with, to touch, what would be your purpose in life? We must discover the joy of each other, the joy of challenge, the joy of growth."[2]

Over the course of a lifetime, most people make about ten thousand acquaintances, but they experience close friendship with only four or five people. The difference between the two is important: with acquaintances there is a lack of transparency, but close friends are vulnerable and caring.

Imagine your circle of friends right now. Some are distant; others speak in clichés or generalities when you're together. But your close friends share their emotions openly. They say, "Here's my life." *These* are chocolate-covered friends.

My hope is that by comparing relationships with the wonderful attributes of chocolate, this book will help you develop richer, deeper, more meaningful friendships.

I can list a number of girlfriends I work with, tramp around antique and craft shows with, travel to retreats with, frequent the same spa and nail shop with, and meet at the park with. I love and enjoy each one. But I *crave* girlfriends who share my beliefs and worldview…who love to think and talk about the meaning of life…who are ready to embrace forgiveness…who are loyal no matter what happens…who are filled with joy. These are my spiritual girlfriends. They're the ones who love the Bible and Jesus with the same enthusiasm and eagerness that bubbles up inside me. They are *chocolate-bearing* friends.

I believe God is preparing someone—perhaps someone you don't know yet—to be your spiritual girlfriend. She may be a member of your church or in your women's Bible study. She may live in your neighborhood or work in your office building. Perhaps she hasn't moved to your town yet, but God is already working in each of your lives to bring you together.

Not long ago I spoke at a women's conference in St. Louis. While I was there, one of the church sponsors, Linda Wallace, said something to me that I'll never forget: "If a woman doesn't have close friends in the church, she will leave the church."[3]

Linda is right. *Friendship matters* in our community of believers. Our love for God connects us, draws us together. It is the advertisement, the billboard, the commercial that says, "God loves you."[4]

My hope is that as you read this book, you will be changed and your friendships will mature. In these pages I will identify nine important ways for you and your girlfriends to survive life's difficulties and enjoy its pleasures:

- Rescuing our friends through communication
- Lending faith when a friend's supply is running low
- Encouraging through words and actions
- Being a "big-time spender"—of time, emotions, and even money
- Forgiving when we are wronged
- Remaining loyal even when rumors run rampant
- Choosing and sharing joy
- Offering the freedom to be authentic and genuine

- Welcoming your girlfriend—not just into your heart, but also into your home

Friends don't preach; they live the sermon. Friends don't lecture on grace; they *are* gracious. Friends don't talk about mercy; they personify it. Friends don't brag about forgiveness; they simply forgive.

And friends offer a warm cup of chocolate to each other in their homes.

If you long for great friendships and crave great chocolate too, this book is for you. So sit back, put your feet up, and start reading. We'll learn about friendship together.

And I'll bring the chocolate.

Chocolate-Covered Lifesavers

Everything I ever needed to know about friendship,
I learned from *I Love Lucy*.
MADELYN PUGH DAVIS

If you can't eat all your chocolate, it will keep in the
freezer. But if you can't eat all your chocolate,
what's wrong with you?
AUTHOR UNKNOWN

Our laughter echoed across the mountain as we hopped off the ski lift and turned toward Paradise Bowl. Shadows danced across the packed snow. At the end of the trail my husband, George, tucked and disappeared, and I followed.

Suddenly it happened: the inside corner of my left ski caught a bump in a glistening patch of ice. Secret fears, long hidden since my first ski lesson years ago, rose in my throat. I gulped and pushed forward, pointing my toes inward—resorting to the awkward stance of the beginner. Then I hit ice again. This time I lost my balance and was thrown headlong into the snow. When I finally rolled to a stop, the pretzel-like twist to my leg confirmed the truth: it was broken.

Someone saw me and began to shout, "Help!" Ski instructors and strangers came running. This put into motion a blur of events. Other skiers retrieved my lost poles and skis, and George hiked up the mountain to assist the ski patrol. As they placed me into the rescue basket, every move sent sharp pain screaming through my body. I was afraid to breathe. All the way down the mountain I prayed—first not to hit a bump, and then to thank God for the rescue.

By the time we returned to Texas, my leg was wrapped hip to toe in a gigantic cast.

And that's when my real lifesavers sprang into action. My girlfriend Kay organized meal deliveries by MOPS members and church friends. My mom came every morning to help with household chores. My daughter Cherry stopped by every day at lunchtime, bringing her special brand of joy and fun. My friend Sue came in the afternoons to pray. After several housebound weeks, my friends Becky and Carol loaded me in a van and took me to a seminar. Handling my wheelchair couldn't have been easy, but their kindness rescued me.

> Chocolate is nature's way of making up for Mondays.
> —AUTHOR UNKNOWN

To top off the blessings, many girlfriends dropped by to deliver chocolate bars, chocolate cookies, and chocolate brownies. It seemed that all of these women, whether I knew them well or had met them only recently, understood the pleasure that chocolate brings to a girl in need.

Chocolate. How sweet it is. As Elaine Sherman once said, "Chocolate causes certain endocrine glands to secrete hormones that affect your feelings and behavior by making you happy. Therefore, it counteracts depression, in turn reducing the stress of depression. Your stress-free life helps you maintain a youthful disposition, both physically and mentally. So, eat lots of chocolate."[1]

In other words, chocolate makes a girl smile.

LIFESAVERS

Yes, I had lifesavers on that mountain—assured, strong, caring professionals who knew just what to do. But what I needed even more were great girlfriends who brought chocolate and spiritual friendship.

Just as it was essential that I be helped down that mountain, so it is vital that we draw support and comfort from other women. We cannot rescue ourselves. We need lifesavers to cling to when we are hurting or about to drown in despair. Lifesavers to pull us to safety when there seems to be no hope. Women who will offer not only advice and assistance, but who will also cover us with love, forgiveness, and friendship—like a shortbread cookie covered in rich, dark, melted chocolate.

While the popular culture touted on television and in magazines urges that we follow our "inner guide" in difficult situations, we know deep down it doesn't work that way. When we live frantic busy lives or stretch ourselves too thin financially or grow weary from health issues or family concerns, we need help. Help from someone outside ourselves. As believers, our first resource is God, who offers unlimited power and strength. No matter what happens, He is available.

But when our struggles shake us to the core and threaten to overwhelm us, we fail to grasp what God offers. We forget how to exercise our faith. We don't automatically embrace the good, noble, or right thing. All too often, we find ourselves tramping around in the muck of self-centeredness, ego, and selfishness.

Self-control mode keeps our minds from grasping the truths found in God's Word. When we are in this mode, nothing seems to reach or encourage us.

Until a girlfriend offers her friendship, that is.

Friendship gives comfort when we are lonely, fierce loyalty when the world believes the worst, freedom to be authentic, encouragement to dream big, and faith when tragedy strikes—all luxurious chocolate coatings from a true girlfriend.

Chocolate symbolizes the luxurious, bountiful, sweet love God enables us to show others. Think I'm a little over the top about chocolate? Consider this verse: "For the Kingdom of God is *not a matter of what we eat or drink*, but of living a life of goodness and peace and joy in the Holy Spirit"[2] (emphasis added).

Godly living isn't sustained by food. But it is supported by a feast of chocolate-covered friendships that help us maneuver through life's mishaps and troubling times.

Take a look at some biblical examples of enduring friendship:

- After Naomi's husband and two grown sons died, her hope was rekindled through her daughter-in-law Ruth.
- David's fears eased thanks to the loyalty and compassion of his best friend, Jonathan.
- Barnabas believed in Paul even when everyone else was suspicious of Paul's motives.
- Paul encouraged Timothy to persevere despite insurmountable difficulties.
- Barnabas accepted Mark when he failed.
- When Moses had no strength left, Aaron and Hur held his arms up.

RELATIONSHIPS NEEDED

In the movie *Crocodile Dundee,* Sue Charlton, a sophisticated, modern, high-fashion New York City journalist, tries to explain to Mick Dundee, a pragmatic outdoorsman from Down Under, that a woman they've just met at a party has been in therapy for years. Sue tells Dundee that therapy is paying a psychiatrist to "listen to your problems and troubles."

After mulling it over, Dundee asks, "What's the matter, doesn't she have any mates?"

We could all use more mates, couldn't we?

We are born with a relationship trigger. As newborns, we want to be held and cuddled. That's the reason a baby will sleep when you hold her but not when she's in her crib.[3] Even when first born, her tiny blue orbs, not fully focusing, nevertheless search for a face. As soon as her eyes connect, your baby soon learns to crook her tiny mouth into a smile. And later, as a toddler, she will watch to see if you are looking at her and bring her toys into the room where you are. Then she will climb up into your lap. Already she is seeking that rich, nurturing, chocolate-covered relationship.

Fame, beauty, and talent are insufficient without true friendship. Popular culture is chock-full of examples of enduring friendships: Ethel loving Lucy, Trixie confiding in Alice, Betty helping Wilma, Mary encouraging Rhoda, Laverne getting into trouble with Shirley, or Monica, Rachel, and Phoebe sharing secrets over coffee.

Throughout our lives we develop friendships. Some are acquaintances and neighbors. Others are friends from the past like those I just saw again at my high-school reunion. We have friends at church, work, and the gym. Some friends are no more than acquaintances. Others vacation together or enjoy the same activities.

But more than anything, we need—*desperately* need—the intimate, rich-as-chocolate accountability of spiritual girlfriends. This is the kind of friend I run to when my world falls flat, the friend I tell my deepest fears and secrets to. This friend offers sympathy before solutions. She is loyal. She doesn't look the other way if I start down a wrong path. I *need* her.

That neediness is real, flowing out of lack, insufficiency, and urgency for connection with a special girlfriend who will open her arms wide, welcoming me home. A girlfriend who will use her ears more than her mouth. Who can share belly-shaking guffaws with me and point me to Jesus because she loves Him as much as I do.

A spiritual girlfriend is one who shares the hope, joy, peace, and understanding that is found in God's Word. A spiritual girlfriend understands the joys and troubles of life, recognizes God's hand in every situation, offers emotional support and spiritual strength, and is always ready to share a bar of chocolate.

Honestly, we don't need more superficial friendships. Don't get me wrong: I love shopping, parties, and trips to the spa, but I *crave* girlfriends who will prod me to make better choices and encourage me to higher heights. Those who will do as the Bible says: "And let us consider how to stimulate one another to love and good deeds."[4]

> Nine out of ten people like chocolate. The tenth person always lies.
> —JOHN Q. TULLIUS

Girlfriends who stimulate each other develop strong faith. Girlfriends who sacrifice of themselves, are willing to forgive, and overflow with loyalty spread joy and freedom to each other with generous hospitality and love. These kinds of girlfriends not only share the lumps of life but also stir up each other's love for God—

and in doing so, offer a depth of friendship that can only be compared to smooth, rich, dark chocolate.

The Bible says, "The LORD is close to the brokenhearted and saves those who are crushed in spirit."[5] Sometimes He is close to us through a girlfriend who is tuned in to Him and willing to be His instrument in our life during a painful, heartbreaking experience.

A signboard on a church near my home asks, "Does your life spread light or cast shadows?" I don't want to be superficial. I don't want to cast any shadows. I don't need any more surface friendships. Let's learn to be spiritual girlfriends.

And I'll bring the chocolate.

OFFERING CHOCOLATE

In friendship, we aren't required to be certified counselors or have a doctoral degree from a seminary. Even without a background in theology, we can help others because we have lived![6] We have experienced life's ups and downs. Some of us have rejoiced in childbirth or struggled in child-raising; others have no children. Some of us are married, some single. Some are widowed. Some have been through divorce. Many have lost a parent, child, sister, or brother.

If you have ever allowed God to minister to you, then you are uniquely equipped to minister to someone else—in effect, to become a chocolate-bearing girlfriend. Every time you experience a success or a failure, you earn the qualification to help someone else. Every time you repent of your sins before Holy God, you grow more equipped to help another person do the same. Because of the joys and sufferings you've been through on your life's journey, you possess skills to help another person.

> Compared to friendship, gold is dirt.
> —AUTHOR UNKNOWN

A chocolate-covered friendship is one that encourages, stimulates hope, and brings out the best in another. The Bible says, "So speak encouraging words to one another. Build up hope so you'll all be together in this, no one left out, no one left behind."[7]

RESCUED

My friend Jeannie tried a new recipe for chocolate–peanut butter brownies. But something went wrong. Her brownies were crumbly and irregular and wouldn't come out of the pan in nice even squares. Instead, she ended up with a plate full of ugly chunks. Since she had planned to take them to an office birthday party, Jeannie panicked.

She quickly called her girlfriend and described the pile of misshapen pieces. Between the two, a restoration plan emerged. Jeannie pulled a pretty glass trifle bowl from her cabinet and went to work. In went a layer of brownie chunks. Then a layer of pudding. Then a layer of peanut butter icing. Layer upon layer, until the bowl was full. Finally she topped the whole thing off with Cool Whip.

It was beautiful.

At the party, everyone raved about Jeannie's delicious dessert and requested her recipe. Jeannie wrote it down and titled it "Rescued Chocolate–Peanut Butter Surprise."

A failed chocolate dessert may not qualify as a major emergency requiring trained troops. But girlfriends—like rescue heroes—respond to emergency calls amid busy schedules with their full attention and creative ideas.

> Nuts just take up space where chocolate ought to be.
> —AUTHOR UNKNOWN

Rescuing others is often risky and requires the use of special tools. A hero offers safety and security and never chooses who he will or won't save. In this way, a true friend is a lot like a chocolate-covered lifesaver. She offers not only help, but also sweetness, love, and joy.

Becoming a chocolate-covered-lifesaver kind of girlfriend means you show up for the good times as well as the messy times. God wants us as Christians to reach out to others, breaking through moods and masks and touching inner souls with fresh hope.

My friend Edith notices my health, happiness, and mood. Sometimes she will say, "You sound stressed. What's up?" Or, "Things must be going your way today! Tell me about it." Her friendship is my chocolate lifesaver. I taste her love and know I don't have to pretend when I am with her. When I run to her in stressful times or cling to her friendship in rejected times, she dishes out friendship like rich chocolate.

Do We Really Know Each Other?

Years ago, families lived in the same area for generations. Grandparents, aunts, uncles, parents, and children were all nearby. The whole town knew the family tree and what accomplishments or troubles faced each family. My Grandmother Addie scandalized the town when she dared to vote. When Addie arrived home, her mother and mother-in-law were waiting on the front porch to discuss proper behavior. Grandmother Addie also bobbed her hair and learned to drive, just to keep everyone alert.

Back in those days, neighborhoods, churches, and schools were like families. Children went to school with the same friends through elementary and secondary school.

Today, urban sprawl and increased mobility means neighborhoods full of people who don't know each other. Even church families don't become acquainted like they used to. Our own church is growing so fast we often don't recognize the people sitting next to us. Our small group meets every week, yet each of us seems to be building a wall around our inner thoughts and struggles.

Helping each other requires getting to know the person

behind the face. *USA Today* reports about how MySpace users "friend" other people on the Internet. Often the person is a total stranger, but that doesn't matter. "Each time [I'm] asked, it feels kinda cool—like *Oh, this person thinks I'm cool enough to befriend me*," says one fifteen-year-old who has more than five thousand friends on her MySpace page. According to *USA Today*, these friends might eventually meet in real life, but more than 90 percent will have virtually no contact with the girl.

Some MySpace users won't befriend someone with less than 150 friends on their personal list because obviously, "No one likes them." Others ignore the list and concentrate on a few real friends.[8]

This kind of interest in making connections isn't new, but technology has changed the playing field from school hallway to computer screen. With the ability to delete an online friend at the touch of a button, friending will never replace friendship— but it does illustrate how much we crave connection with others.

Becoming a chocolate-bearing friend requires knowing the details about each other and begins with learning to communicate at deep levels.

UNWRAPPING THE COMMUNICATION CANDY BAR

Communication often begins with a friendly "How are you?" and the response "Fine, how are you?" This might lead to "Nice weather we are having," followed by "Yes, I hope it doesn't rain this weekend." Conversations like these often conclude with phrases such as "Have a nice day" and "Take care."

I call this first stage of communication the Candy Bar Wrapper Level. When you buy a candy bar, the first thing you're drawn to is the pretty, well-designed wrapper. In the same way, this stage of communication consists of surface chitchat that is positive, pleasant, and enticing, but it doesn't reveal the deliciousness inside.

The second stage is the Nutrition Panel Level. Like the nutrition panel on the back of a candy wrapper, this level offers the who, what, when, where, why, and how. At this point in the conversation, you might ask, "How many children do you have?" or "Where did you grow up?" The facts and figures are analyzed and absorbed. This step offers the information you need to learn more about the other person.

> Chocolate is cheaper than therapy and you don't need an appointment.
> —AUTHOR UNKNOWN

Stage three is the Unwrap the Candy Bar Level. This stage scratches the surface of our inner thoughts by inviting deeper communication. Just as you unwrap a candy bar to see the treasure inside, this step allows you to share your thoughts with another: "I feel like my life is moving too fast," or "I think he's the best candidate because…" To become chocolate lifesavers for each other, we have to move to a deeper communication level.

Stage four is the Heart Level. Like inhaling the luscious aroma of the chocolate inside, as this stage happens you grow comfortable enough to say, "Tell me how you feel," or "I'm disappointed because…" This is the stage when you express your feelings and open up emotionally.

And finally, stage five—the Truth Talk Level. Like finally placing the candy bar in our mouths and savoring the wonder of the chocolate, this intimate level of communication allows you to trust another by sharing how you feel. This is the stage where you accept each other's faults and failures, where you say, "I love you for who you are and not for what you do"—and *mean* it. This is where you lay your hand on a friend's shoulder and tell her, "It's okay. Everyone makes mistakes."

Not all friends will move with you to the level of Truth Talk. Some people don't feel safe there. It is difficult, for example, to develop an intimate friendship with someone who doesn't share your commitment to Jesus. And just as too many chocolate bars aren't healthy, so will only a few friends ever reach the highest level of intimacy with you. But don't let this limitation discourage you. It is possible, through honesty and openness, to develop more spiritual friendships than you ever dared imagine.

In my small Bible study group, we meet weekly, share a meal, and discuss a rich lesson from the Bible. We build relationships and friendships. But it isn't in our nature to readily expose the rough places of life to a group unless each has invested time and honesty. Only after years of meeting together did Glen share with us about his son's struggle with drugs. No one had known. It took a long time for him to trust our group with such private information.

As we offered him our love, concern, and prayers without judgment, our small group moved into a new stage of transparency. Soon afterward, another person shared a deep struggle. And then another.

Glen took a huge risk, but it opened a door for others to embrace honesty and become vulnerable as well. The apostle Paul explained this intimate level of communication when he wrote, "We loved you so much that we were delighted to share with you not only the gospel of God but our lives as well, because you had become so dear to us."[9]

Truth Talk is never superficial. It goes deep beneath the surface to bring us person to person, sometimes gut to gut. Not everyone is capable or willing to commit to this deep level of intimacy, but those who do discover amazing friendship. If I share with you my doubts and admit my deep, not-so-lovely feelings, and you share your hurts and hopes with me, we develop bonds that can't compare to any surface relationship.

The Truth Talk level of communication is where we acknowledge our weaknesses and admit our fears. That's when we can ask for help, when we can pray specifically and fervently for each other.

Moving beyond surface communication begins with the safety of unconditional love. Intimacy develops as we share how we think and feel, and it blossoms when we let God lead us into unforgettable friendships. Spiritual depth, rescuing, caring friends, and Truth Talk are the ingredients for true friendships—the chocolate-lifesaver kind.

Bringing the Chocolate

1. Make a list of friends that you know only on the Candy Bar Wrapper level. One by one, invite each of them into your home for a meal or for coffee and dessert (something chocolate, of course!). You'll discover family backgrounds and encourage each other's dreams as you talk together.

2. Ask a girlfriend how she came to know the Lord Jesus Christ.

3. Begin a small group with the goal of meeting weekly or bimonthly. As you share together, develop level-five communication.

4. Start a book club and choose Christian books, non-fiction or fiction. Ask each person to come prepared to discuss what they learned or felt.

Prayer

Dear Lord, I ask you to put people who need a chocolate life-saver into my path. Please make me aware of who they are.

Offering Chocolate to My Friend

Dear friend, I commit myself to be your
chocolate-covered lifesaver.

Chocolate-Covered Life Savers

*You've probably been reading this chapter wondering how
chocolate-covered Life Savers would taste. Maybe you can't imagine
mixing the two flavors. Try this easy, fun recipe and you may just
fall in love with Chocolate-Covered Life Savers for dessert.*

Ingredients:

1 roll of mixed-flavor Life Savers

1 cup real white chocolate chips

10 Hershey's chocolate bars (4-oz size), without nuts

1 cup dark chocolate chips (optional)

Directions:

Open the roll of Life Savers and separate the flavors into individual sealable bags. Use a rolling pin to crush the Life Savers into small pieces. Set aside.

Melt the white chocolate chips by placing them in a clean, dry glass bowl and microwaving on high for one minute, then stirring until smooth. If necessary, microwave in additional ten-second increments until melted and smooth.

Cut the Hershey's chocolate bars in half. Lay one on a sheet of waxed paper. Spread melted white chocolate over it and then sprinkle with pieces of Life Savers. Repeat with the remaining chocolate bars. Allow the candy to cool until the white chocolate hardens (place in the refrigerator for quicker results). Enjoy!

Optional decoration: Melt the dark chocolate chips (see above). Transfer the melted chocolate to a Ziploc bag and snip a small hole in the corner. Pipe a ribbon of chocolate in a crisscross design over the cooled bars.

Chocolate-Frosted Yellow Layer Cake Faith

Walking with a friend in the dark
is better than walking alone in the light.
HELEN KELLER

Put "eat chocolate" at the top of your list of things to do
today. That way, at least you'll get one thing done.
AUTHOR UNKNOWN

My mother makes a yellow layer cake with an amazing chocolate-fudge icing. If you saw it, you'd probably wonder why I call it "amazing"—because it is never pretty! In fact, our family has dubbed it "the ugly cake."

Instead of standing up in fluffy swirls, her frosting is hard and somewhat lumpy. Mother doesn't follow a recipe or have a definable technique for her icing. She simply stirs up some ingredients and cooks it until it looks right, and then she pours it on the cake. Sometimes it flows freely over the layers and forms a smooth covering, but other times it clumps up too soon and barely covers the cake. Mother never knows what will happen.

But no one in the family cares. We can't wait to get a slice because we know the flavor will be delicious. We have faith in the promise of the cake no matter how it looks.

Because our family has grown, Mom now makes two cakes so that everyone gets a slice. In fact, we fight over the corner pieces (did you know you can get four or more corner pieces from a round cake?) because those pieces have the most icing. Mom's grandson Munroe even wanted ugly cake for the groom's cake at his and Leslie's wedding…and Mom made it for him. It didn't look like a professional bakery cake, but as soon as the reception started and the first person to try it spread the word, guests gathered around the table to make sure they got a slice.

> I don't understand why so many so-called chocolate lovers complain about the calories in chocolate, when all true chocoholics know that it is a vegetable. It comes from the cocoa bean, beans are veggies, 'nuff said.
>
> —AUTHOR UNKNOWN

Ugly cake is not made to look at; it is made to be shared and enjoyed. In the same way, when we have an assured and confident faith, its richness draws our friends into our hearts and offers sweet comfort and help.

LENDING FAITH

Pam and Ken tried everything to conceive a baby, but medical problems prevented them from getting pregnant. It was hard to give up their dream of having a biological family, but after praying and talking, they decided to look into adoption.

Years of home studies, personality profiles, and questionnaires followed, and their hope for an adopted baby became as real and precious as their hope for a birth child had been. Finally, after painting their nursery and putting together the crib, adoption day arrived. Pam loaded the new diaper bag, car seat, and an outfit for the new baby into the car just as the telephone rang.

> Everyone has to believe in something. I believe I'll have some more chocolate.
> —AUTHOR UNKNOWN

"We are so sorry, but the birth mother has changed her mind. She wants to keep her baby," the adoption agency manager said.

In that single moment, Pam's dream disintegrated. *Why is God letting this happen?*

When I heard Pam and Ken's news, I drove straight to their house. Pam sat in a recliner, an afghan pulled up to her eyes. I didn't know what to do, so I sat on the sofa and silently prayed, *Father, Pam's faith has been wounded today. She is devastated. Since her faith wavers just now and mine is strong, I ask You to lend her my faith.*

I knew that someday, after the numbing shock, gut-wrenching pain, and grief had worn off, Pam's faith would grow strong and robust again. Her trust in God would be renewed following this unthinkable heartbreak. But I also knew that today Pam was on an emotional roller coaster—climbing to a peak in anticipation of the baby, then plunging headlong into grief. Her mind was in turmoil. She questioned God, wondering why He had allowed her pain. She might even be speculating about His ability to keep His promises or trying to think up a reason for this punishment or begging God for a sign that He loved her.

During those hours of agony, I asked God to lend her my faith—until hers had recovered.

I never told anyone about my prayer. Many years later, Pam and I talked about that dreadful day. She remembered that I didn't quote Scripture or try to offer a solution. She told me, "I can still see you sitting on that sofa. I looked at you and felt braver because of your strong faith."

God had answered my quiet prayer. When Pam's faith weakened, I held strong so she wouldn't lose hope. In those hours of grief, God allowed me to offer a slice of chocolate-laced faith to Pam.

When friends experience disasters, death, sickness, or financial problems, we can slice off a piece of our strong faith and offer it to them at a time when their faith is at its weakest. Pastor and author Rick Warren said, "When circumstances crush us to the point that our faith falters, that's when we need believing friends the most."[1]

THE CENTURION'S FAITH

Matthew reports that an important military officer cared enough for his sick servant to walk a long distance to find healing grace from Jesus. This centurion recognized authority and power in Jesus. In fact, in the original manuscripts, the Greek word that the centurion used to ask for healing indicates that he asked for the impossible. No more medical treatments; he wanted a miracle.

> When Jesus had entered Capernaum, a centurion came to him, asking for help. "Lord," he said, "my servant lies at home paralyzed and in terrible suffering."
>
> Jesus said to him, "I will go and heal him."
>
> The centurion replied, "Lord, I do not deserve to have you come under my roof. But just say the word, and my servant will be healed. For I myself am a man under authority, with soldiers under me. I tell this one, 'Go,' and he goes; and that one, 'Come,' and he comes. I say to my servant, 'Do this,' and he does it."
>
> When Jesus heard this, he was astonished and said to those following him, "I tell you the truth, I have not found anyone in Israel with such great faith."[2]

The centurion's strong faith compelled him to bring another person's problems to Jesus. His faith built a bridge for someone else. His faith astonished Jesus.

How can you and I share slices of our faith? How can we develop faith that would astonish Jesus?

DON'T THROW AWAY YOUR CONFIDENCE

Nothing is quite as elegant or delicious as a homemade three-layer cake. Just as a good cake requires confidence in your ingredients and cooking skills, strong faith requires confidence in what you believe in and hope for. Do you want to become a friend who can lend faith to someone who feels isolated from God? Like gathering quality ingredients to make a chocolate layer cake, you need to start by searching out the truths revealed in God's Word. The book of Hebrews tells us,

> Remember those earlier days after you had received the
> light, when you stood your ground in a great contest in
> the face of suffering. Sometimes you were publicly exposed
> to insult and persecution; at other times you stood side by
> side with those who were so treated.... So do not throw
> away your confidence; it will be richly rewarded.[3]

Did you notice the phrase "So do not throw away your confidence"? When I first read those words, I realized that I can either be confident in the power of God or I can let my confidence go. Astonishing faith depends on my willingness to cling to and get a grip on my belief.

Confidence is the essence of faith. True faith relies on God because it acknowledges that He is in control. Not self-assurance; *God-assurance*. Confidence!

God tells us to be confident in two things: what we hope for and what we do not see. According to the Bible, hope is not "hope so." Instead, hope is the certain and unshakable belief that God holds the future in His capable hand.

Our friend Milo Hamilton invited George and me to watch the sunrise on Haleakala, the giant mountain on Maui. The driver came to our hotel at three in the morning so we could reach the volcano's summit during the predawn darkness. When we arrived, we found more than five hundred people sitting along the side of a hill facing east. We found our spot and waited. And waited. Not one

> There are four basic food groups: milk chocolate, dark chocolate, white chocolate, and chocolate truffles.
> —AUTHOR UNKNOWN

person in the crowd gave up the vigil, even though we waited a long time. Not one person climbed back into the car thinking that the sun wouldn't come up that day. We all waited because we knew that soon the eastern sky would brighten. We waited with hope. Finally we saw the first rays shoot through the clouds. Then a tiny sliver of the sun peeked over the horizon.

Real faith believes what it cannot see. If I can see something, I don't need faith to believe it. Real faith believes just "because God said so." God delights in a person who believes in Him (Hebrews 11:6). Real faith doesn't make an inventory of what God will provide. Rather, real faith knows that God will provide the right thing, in the right amount, at just the right time. As Paul told the Corinthians, "So we fix our eyes not on what is seen, but on what is unseen. For what is seen is temporary, but what is unseen is eternal."[4]

KNOWING WHAT YOU BELIEVE
BUILDS LAYERS OF FAITH

I sometimes wonder how anyone can go through life without knowing what to believe or, worse, just searching for something "out there" and never finding the truth. Their lives must feel miserable and incomplete. Knowing what we believe helps us be strong, mature women. We can be true friends to other women when we possess this kind of maturity. If we are shaky and unsure, our friendships suffer. Chocolate sharers need the maturity of knowing what we believe.

All my life I depended on how much I worked in the church to give me confidence in God. You name the battle, and I've tried to be a soldier. But I never really rested in my faith. I knew the doctrines of my church; I kept them in my arsenal in case I needed to prove a point or make an argument. Using my beliefs like weapons left me with weak, sometimes faltering faith. I doubted whether all my activity and work was enough. I was uncertain and skeptical, like John the Baptist, who said, "Are You the one?" or the disciples, who asked, "Don't You care?" or Mary, who cried, "If only You had been here."

My friend Bobbie Russell taught a community Bible study that didn't focus on the minute details of doctrines but instead emphasized the glorious truths of God and the plan that He implemented to save our wretched souls. One night she spoke about the resurrection:

> What effect does the resurrection have on your life?
> His dying paid the debt, and His resurrection defeated
> death. Because of His mercy and grace in this act of
> unquestionable love, He is our God and all His power is
> ours. The key to living a victorious life is to yield to His
> unquestionable love.[5]

Her challenge to yield penetrated my know-it-all shell, and I realized faith had nothing to do with effort. I didn't have to perform to please God. Instead, I should stand aside, give Him the lead, and follow.

Two things will keep our faith strong. The first strength is built on our experiences with God—when we see His hand at work in life situations. The disciples who followed Jesus into Cana witnessed the miracle of the wine at the wedding. In performing this miracle, Jesus first began to reveal Himself. At that moment, the initial sparks of faith were ignited in them.

Each time we see God work, our faith grows. The first time the disciples saw Jesus calm a storm on the sea, they wondered who He could be.[6] The second time He stilled the winds, they said, "Truly, you are the Son of God."[7] Their faith grew from one storm to the next.

My friend Sherry needed a tree removed from her property, but finances were tight. Then a county cleanup crew came along and removed the tree at no charge because it grew on the county right-of-way.

When God shows up, our faith increases.

The second strength flows from the valuable biblical principles that we learn when we read the Bible. I've gathered a block of beliefs—basic truths straight from the Bible—that fit together just like the ingredients for a cake. Scholars call these beliefs "core dogma" or "orthodoxy." These doctrines, such as the deity of Christ, the virgin birth, and the resurrection, are the fundamentals of Christianity. It is important to understand the basics.

> Strength is the capacity to break a chocolate bar into four pieces with your bare hands—and then eat just one of the pieces.
> —JUDITH VIORST

I have discovered that several of these doctrines are like the layers of a cake. When the layers are stacked together, my confidence is strong. If my life is in disarray, I remember these essentials and secure my confidence in them.

LAYER NUMBER ONE—CREATED BY GOD

God created everything. He mixes the ingredients for all life.

I don't understand what my husband, the science teacher, understands about science. (I don't even want to understand what he understands.) With Creation, however, no one will ever know the how of Creation; but we do know the Who of Creation. The Bible says, "By faith we understand that the universe was formed at God's command, so that what is seen was not made out of what was visible."[8]

God existed at the beginning. In fact, He existed before the beginning. Pastor S. M. Lockridge said this in a classic sermon about creation:

> God was all there was. God called light out of darkness.
> God called peace out of chaos. God called order out of
>   confusion.
> And He came from nowhere!
> *The reason He had to come from nowhere is because there*
>   *wasn't anywhere for Him to come from.*

Coming from nowhere—He stood on nothing.

The reason He stood on nothing is because there wasn't
anywhere for Him to stand.

He reached out—when there was nowhere to reach and
caught something when there was nothing to catch.
And He hung that something on nothing and told it
to stay there!

Standing on nothing, He took the hammer of His own will
and struck the anvil of His omnipotence and sparks
flew there from. He caught the sparks on the tips of
His fingers and bedecked the heavens with stars.

And nobody said a word!

*The reason no one said anything was because there wasn't
anybody there to say anything!*

So God Himself said, "That's good!"[9]

Ask yourself: Are you convinced God created the universe?
Are you sure God created you? Do you believe it? If so, then you
can live through any turmoil or trouble with confidence because
the Creator of all things has everything under control. If we are
confident God will take bad and make it good, then we have a
foundation.

Extraordinary friendships—the kind of friendships that can
offer chocolate-layer-cake faith to others—believe that God cre-
ates and sustains life.

LAYER NUMBER TWO—JESUS CHRIST DIED IN MY PLACE

The Bible says God created us and that He loves us like no one else could: "But God demonstrates his own love for us in this: While we were still sinners, Christ died for us."[10]

We are sinners, hopeless and helpless. We cannot approach a holy God in our sins. The Bible says we deserve severe punishment. Death. Jesus took our penalty when He died on the cross. Then He rose again, victorious over death. He offers that same resurrected, abundant life to you and me—if we believe. Jesus said, "I tell you the truth, whoever hears my word and believes him who sent me has eternal life and will not be condemned; he has crossed over from death to life."[11]

> I can trust my friends. These people force me to examine myself, encourage me to grow.
> —CHER

Trouble and tragedy may shake our faith, but if the ingredients are mixed according to God's recipe, a recipe that includes how much God loves us (so much that He left His throne in heaven to rescue us), our faith won't collapse. The question is, *If God made that sacrifice for me, can I trust Him not to ignore my pain or sorrow?* If you can trust Him totally, you will be able to offer chocolate to others.

Two faith layers—God the creator and sustainer of life and God who chose to die in our place—make it possible for us to lend strength and courage to girlfriends.

LAYER NUMBER THREE—INTIMACY WITH GOD

I came face to face with my need for intimacy with God a few years ago. I became a Christ follower in childhood, and I worked hard at my Christianity. I thought the more things I did, the more God loved me. Every week I participated wholeheartedly in at least three worship services, sang in the choir, and performed solos and ensemble music. I never missed Sunday school and often taught classes for children or teens.

At church events, I filled glasses with ice, washed dishes, and served with enthusiasm. And when revival or VBS or workshops came along, you could always find me in the second row, left-hand side, a smile in place. My social circle consisted of Christian friends. No matter what the Christian occasion, I joined in. My life was "all about me."

Frankly, I felt happy and proud of myself. I never realized how shallow my life was. Never knew about an intimate relationship with Jesus Christ. Then I heard about a community Bible study. And with my get-in-there-and-serve attitude, I soon joined the leadership team.

But two things surprised me about the leadership group. First, we met at 6:30 in the morning. *Saturday morning.* There was something unusual about these gals.

Second, we prayed. Of course, I had anticipated that we would pray, so I planned what to say, imagining that my words would inspire and uplift the other leaders. They would realize the strength of my Christianity and admire my oratory skills.

Did I mention how shallow and self-centered I was?

But these gals didn't pray long prayers aloud. Instead, one by one, each woman slid from her chair to her knees. In no particular order, each spoke simple, short sentences of praise and thanksgiving.

"Thank You, Lord, for being our Creator."

"Praise You for the gift of sunshine."

"Praise You for Your salvation."

"Thank You for giving us life."

"Praise You for Your Word."

On and on they went. No preplanned oratory, no formula, no flowery words. Finally it dawned on me: *these gals are talking to God like He's an old friend.*

These women, who came from different denominations and did not hold all my same strict notions, dogma, or theological minutiae, possessed something I didn't: a growing, authentic relationship with Jesus.

During those predawn Saturday sessions, something happened to the pride, accomplishments, busy calendar, and hard-nosed stands on meaningless issues that had for so long made up my recipe for Christianity. A new intimacy with God changed the old recipe of service-shows-how-good-I-am to an up-close, personal friendship with Jesus.

Unless we are intimate with God, we cannot lend faith to our girlfriends. When we add intimacy with God to our recipe, He works for our best, and then we can relay our trust to our girlfriends who are pained or sorrowful.

THE IMPORTANCE OF FAITH

My life, like yours, is busy and frantic. Many days I stumble around as if there is nothing to cling to. If I stop long enough to consider these three strong layers in the cake of faith, I can lean on these three things: God created and sustains all things; Jesus Christ took the death penalty and offers life; and each individual can experience intimacy with God.[12]

Why should we understand what we believe? Because problems are on their way. Difficulties are just ahead. When a leader in our church admitted to an affair involving another church member, my faith was assaulted by doubt. I considered giving up, abandoning Christianity or at least the church. But as the details unfolded, I looked into my heart and found that my layer cake of faith was still fully intact. I could forgive and move on.

> Chocolate-covered raisins, cherries, orange slices, and strawberries all count as fruit, so eat as many as you want.
> —AUTHOR UNKNOWN

It wasn't easy. Feelings had been hurt. Pedestals were suddenly vacant, and disappointment nearly strangled me. But I drew strength from my core belief. Those facts that I had determined to be true, no matter what, gave me courage during a time of doubt and uncertainty.

Two of my girlfriends needed me desperately during this time. One was a new Christian who needed the reassurance that God was real and that all Christians weren't frauds. She needed to know that I wasn't pretending and that I truly believed. As she and I talked and cried, I offered her slices of confidence and hope because I knew the biblical principles were true.

The second friend who needed me was the wife of that church leader. Her world literally fell apart. She needed practical help to function—car maintenance, moving, gathering important papers, selling home appliances and furniture. Reminders to eat. She also needed emotional support. She cried until there were no more tears. I reminded her to breathe. And spiritual strength, which I could only offer if my faith-laced layers were in place and ready.

When we meet trouble head-on, the strength of our faith radiates to our girlfriends and causes their faith to grow. Like chocolate icing between each layer, our faith is held together by love and compassion. If I am strong in my faith, I am able to offer my friend my strength.

With those layers stacked firmly together and coated with love and mercy, God will use me to bring Him close to a girlfriend whose heart is broken. Isaiah the prophet said, "The Spirit of the Sovereign LORD is on me, because the LORD has anointed me to preach good news to the poor. He has sent me to bind up the brokenhearted, to proclaim freedom for the captives and release from darkness for the prisoners."[13]

You may not think your faith is all that strong. I don't feel strong in my faith either, but what we must remember is that faith is a process. Just as baking a cake begins with mixing ingredients together, so faith continues to be a journey away from the theology of "me, me, me" to a recipe with God as the Great Mixer who combines a smidgen of belief and a cup of doubt with a pound of Bible study and a pinch of prayer.

My faith is stronger than it used to be, but not as strong as it will be if I stop making myself the object of my faith and concentrate on Christ Jesus Himself. As you add each tiny pinch of faith to your personal recipe, God will strengthen you into a person of strong faith layers.

Faith unlocks the mysteries of Christian living. Faith pleases God. The Bible says, "And without faith it is impossible to please God, because anyone who comes to him must believe that he exists and that he rewards those who earnestly seek him."[14]

STRENGTH FROM A FRIEND

When I broke my leg in that skiing accident, I couldn't walk, but soon my other leg became stronger so that I could stand with my crutches. My arms gained strength as I used them to pull myself around. My other body parts tried to make up for the broken part until it mended.

When trouble strikes a friend, it requires the rest of us to be stronger than ever. We become strong legs and arms holding her up until she can walk again. Remember that Truth Talk is how we know she needs help, and our strong faith is what we offer her.

When God seems far away, a friend with deep faith brings Him closer. The Bible says, "A despairing man should have the devotion of his friends, even though he forsakes the fear of the Almighty."[15]

How to Lend My Faith

Our actions determine whether we truly believe God or not. When we know God keeps His promises and will take care of us, we take no doubtful steps. We say with the prophet, "Ah, Sovereign LORD, you have made the heavens and the earth by your great power and outstretched arm. Nothing is too hard for you."[16]

In Acts, the apostle Paul demonstrated how to lend faith to others who are distressed when he sailed to Rome on a prisoner ship. A storm swept through the Mediterranean Sea, and the ship took a violent battering. The sailors threw cargo and tackle overboard. They tied ropes around the hull. With no stars or moon to navigate, they were lost at sea. After many days, with vanishing food and little hope, Paul told the sailors that God had promised they would be safe. Then Paul did an unusual thing. He held bread up. He said, "Keep your courage, men, for I have faith in God."[17]

When survival seemed impossible, Paul stood strong in his faith. With no hope of rescue, Paul thanked God for provision. When food supplies dwindled, he said, "Let's eat." When the storm got worse, Paul believed God's hand could control storms, and Paul stood strong with his faith. I like to think the loaf of bread Paul held aloft was his own personal version of a chocolate layer cake.

Faith is vision to see what God is going to do. Hope is the present enjoyment of future blessings.[18] Paul knew the ship was in trouble, but his solid faith helped him believe in God's safe reality beyond the storm.

When they reached shore, the prisoner Paul took charge, giving direction, comfort, and encouragement. Paul lent his faith to the sailors when theirs reached the weakest point.

Believing is not just a matter of words; it involves the way we live. Is your faith strong enough for those around you? Can you lift bread, or chocolate, before a starving girlfriend? Do you know what you believe? If so, you'll build chocolate-layer-cake friendships. Everything else is just icing.

Bringing the Chocolate

1. Describe to a close friend at least one major belief that you would never compromise.
2. Make a list of your personal, essential beliefs. Be sure to list scriptures that support or confirm those beliefs.
3. Recall a time when your faith was shattered but the strong faith of another Christian gave you strength. Call that person today to say thank you.
4. Discuss with a small group of friends how one person's strong faith can be a sweet relief to others.

Prayer

Dear Lord, help me lend my faith to others like rich, comforting slices of chocolate layer cake.

Offering Chocolate to My Friend

Dear friend, I'll lend you my faith when you can't see God.

Nanny's Ugly Cake

Just as building a faith layer cake takes time and effort, making Nanny's ugly cake will take a lot of practice. I've tried and failed many times. Sometimes my icing is so thin it runs off the cake plate onto the counter. Other times it's so stiff I can't get it out of the mixing bowl and onto the cake. I complained to Mother about how hard it is to make, and she told me she had failed hundreds of times too. Since she's been making the cake for more than fifty years, she now enjoys mostly success. I made up my mind not to give up trying because when the icing works, it is the most delicious and wonderful chocolate delight you'll ever taste. I've made the recipe more scientific and easier by adding instructions using a candy thermometer. I have tested the thermometer technique over and over, and it works. So give it a try and enjoy!

Ingredients:

1 box yellow cake mix (along with whatever additional ingredients are called for in the directions on the back of the box)

2 teaspoons pure vanilla extract

Directions:

Mix the contents of the cake mix according to instructions on the box. Fold in the vanilla, then pour into two or three pre-greased round layer pans. Bake according to directions; cool on a wire rack.

Icing:

1/4 cup unsweetened cocoa (not Dutch process)

1 1/2 cups granulated sugar

Dash salt

3/4 cup evaporated milk

2 tablespoons unsalted butter

1 teaspoon pure vanilla extract

Combine cocoa, sugar, and salt in a large saucepan. Stir in milk and cook over medium heat until the mixture is thick and boiling. Boil until it reaches 230°F on a candy thermometer. Remove from heat, add butter and vanilla, and beat with mixer until shiny and smooth.

Frost the cooled cake layers immediately by covering each layer with icing and stacking together. Pour the remaining icing over the top and sides.

Chocolate-Kiss Encouragement

All you really need is love, but a little chocolate now and
then doesn't hurt.
Lucy Van Pelt, *PEANUTS*

Two are better than one, because they have a good return
for their work: If one falls down, his friend can help him
up. But pity the man who falls and has no one to help
him up!
Ecclesiastes 4:9–10

*A*s a college freshman, I watched my friend struggle with a
world history course. Despite the fact that she was valedictorian of her high school, she barely squeezed out a C in Pro-
fessor Anderson's intense and demanding classroom.

Since I had not been valedictorian, I avoided the class.
Instead, I took the summer course at my hometown community
college. Summer classes are intense—three hours a night, three
nights a week—and cover a full semester's work in a few weeks.
Then I missed three days of class, the equivalent of three weeks'
work *(yes, youth camp was way more fun than summer school)*. The

next Monday, a friend said, "Tonight we will be tested on the material presented while you were gone."

I worried. I wanted to give up.

I sat on the ottoman at the foot of my father's favorite chair and told him my dilemma. "I've decided to drop the class."

He removed his reading glasses and looked at me with his clear blue eyes. "Karen, why don't you read the textbook? Then take the test tonight. If you fail, I'll let you drop the class. If you do well, you can finish the course."

I could give up chocolate, but I'm not a quitter.
—AUTHOR UNKNOWN

I studied hard, passed the test, and finished the semester with a B. Those few encouraging words from my father gave me the boost I needed.

Dad's encouragement, like a solid milk-chocolate kiss, proved his love for me through and through. His confidence in me never changed, never wavered. And his advice helped me through a difficult situation. Good thing, because during the second summer semester at that community college, I met my future husband, George, and we were married a year later. Without my daddy's gentle push, I would have quit school and not been there to meet my husband.

Encouragement can change your life.

Chocolate kisses now come in dozens of styles and flavors. Some are solid milk chocolate; others are filled with nuts; one type is a combination of swirled dark and white chocolate; and the new-comer is coated in a hard candy covering.

Encouragement, I've found, is like a chocolate-candy kiss. Even a small piece yields a wonderful result, and we find our-selves looking forward eagerly to the next taste. In the same way, just a word of encouragement hints at the deep love of a friend and leaves us wanting more.

Mary Lincoln, granddaughter of Abraham Lincoln, owned a small box containing the contents of the president's pockets on the night of his assassination. In the box was a "Letters to the Edi-tor" section from a newspaper, folded and worn. One of the let-ters in the section praised President Lincoln for all his successes and his singleness of purpose.

As it turns out, everyone—even President Abe Lincoln—needs encouragement.[1] In other words, man doesn't live by bread alone; he needs a little buttering up.

EVERYONE NEEDS ENCOURAGEMENT

One of the best ways to define encouragement is "hope." When we have hope we are not discouraged. When we have hope, the future is brighter. When we have hope, life takes on a new meaning.

You may think you don't have much hope right now. Maybe your health is bad, or the health of a loved one is threatened. Maybe you've lost your spouse, and you feel alone. Maybe your finances are in a mess, and you don't see any way out. The future looks bleak. But there is great reason to be encouraged if you are a Christ follower. For us, hope is the assurance that God is in control. It is the contentment promised in the book of Hebrews. We can rest in God and hope in God because He is trustworthy.

I recently read a novel set in nineteenth-century England. A horseback-riding accident had blinded one of the characters, and the doctors had covered the man's eyes and prescribed complete rest. In the beginning he prayed constantly for God to give him his sight back, but he eventually came to the conclusion that even if he stayed blind the rest of his life, he could trust God. He believed that whatever God planned was the best plan, blind or with sight.

That's hope. Hope is putting faith to work when doubting would be easier. And when we understand that kind of hope, we can be encouraged ourselves and offer the same encouragement to others.

The Bible says that if we "take hold of the hope offered to us [we will] be greatly encouraged. We have this hope as an anchor for the soul, firm and secure."[2] I like to visualize that verse as if we could reach up and grab a handful of hope just before walking out the door each morning. That handful of hope encourages me to face whatever the day throws at me.

God created this world, and He is still in charge. There is hope because God is in control. He has good, not evil, planned for your life (see Jeremiah 29:11). He loves you with an everlasting love. *Nothing* is impossible with God. So be encouraged. It is important for us to be encouraged in our faith and then become an encourager to those around us.

One of the unmistakable signs that a person is a true Christ follower is the existence of a love that desires to help others—a love that wants to minister and encourage even if it costs something. Your negative words and your pessimistic outlook can keep someone else stuck. If you only tell someone what is wrong, they will never grasp hope. If you focus on what's inconveniencing you, you will never be happy and you'll make everyone around you miserable too.

Not long ago I visited a large metropolitan church. A media scandal involving a well-known public personality in another church had recently sent negative shockwaves throughout the Christian community. But instead of adding to the condemnation, Pastor Steve Riggle prayed for the man. His words of encouragement changed my views and my attitude about the news reports.

During a writers' conference at Glen Eyrie, the fabulous castle-hotel outside Colorado Springs, attendees were encouraged to read their work aloud to others in a café setting one evening. The emcee instructed us to listen and to offer critiques to the author. His instructions were simple: for every phrase of criticism, there should be a corresponding phrase of encouragement. That night, the air was filled with hope for both novices and seasoned writers.

Because I hold an executive position and am required to project confidence and poise, it is often difficult for others to believe that I have insecurities. But the wavering, wobbly person deep inside me often surfaces in private. My friend Georgia Shaffer, author of the book *A Gift of Mourning Glories: Restoring Your Life After Loss*, sees beyond my doubts and forces me to look there too. She often tells me, "Karen, that's the Enemy worming his way into your mind. Don't let him do it. You are capable and talented." Her words of encouragement propel me past hesitancy, indecision, and procrastination.

Your friend may look like she has it all together, but look beyond that facade because everyone needs encouragement.

DARK-CHOCOLATE ENCOURAGEMENT

David lived in danger and fear because Saul, the king, followed hot on his trail and intended to kill him. "While David was at Horesh in the Desert of Ziph, he learned that Saul had come out to take his life." And then something amazing happened: "And Saul's son Jonathan went to David at Horesh and helped him find strength in God."[3]

Jonathan, the heir to the throne, chose to encourage David instead of follow in his father's evil plans. Jonathan didn't find a cave for David to hide in, nor did he soothe his friend with plat-itudes and empty promises. He encouraged David to find his strength in God, the only true stronghold.

Encouragement that exposes God's hand in a situation is the deepest kind of friendship. That's what we should offer our girl-friends. Florence Littauer, international speaker, author, and trainer of Christian communicators, is a master encourager. I once observed her with an emotionally distraught woman who was hovering around the perimeter of the room. Most of us were uncomfortable and didn't know what to do (truthfully, we wished she'd disappear). Instead of brush-ing the woman aside, Flor-ence put her arms around her and prayed aloud. Peace filled the room as Florence pointed the woman to Jesus and asked for His intervention. The woman walked away with her head held high and her hope restored because Florence poured lavish encouragement on her. With that simple action, Florence taught me volumes.

> Other things are just food. But chocolate's a beneficent restorer of exhausted power. It is the best friend of those engaged in literary pursuits.
> —BARON JUSTUS VON LIEBIG, GERMAN CHEMIST
> (1803–1873)

That's the kind of encouragement Jonathan gave to David by pointing him to the Source of all strength. David escaped Saul's clutches and eventually became king.

Both Jonathan and Florence are like rich, dark-chocolate

kisses; the sumptuous encouragement they offer points others to God—the only true Source of help.

Encouraging words build up others. Encouraging words offer hope. Encouraging words point the needy to Jesus, put the hand of the lonely into God's hand, point a friend in the right direction.

SAYING "I CARE"—LIKE A CHOCOLATE KISS WITH AN ALMOND INSIDE

A few simple words can energize a grieving soul. When I learned that my father had died, our pastor, Dee Black, said to me, "Karen, I don't know how you feel, but I care how you feel."

Dee's words comforted and encouraged me through the ordeal of my father's funeral and burial. They rang in my ears over and over. Filled with grief and pain, I carried that little snippet of truth with me: *someone cares.*

Today, over twenty years later, I still remember that feeling of encouragement. Dee could have quoted Scripture; he could have reminded me that death always follows life; he could have encouraged me to celebrate my heritage from my godly father; he could have performed some practical deed for our family. Any of these things would have been helpful, kind, and loving. But saying that he cared encouraged me the most.

Dee's rich, caring words were like a chocolate kiss with an almond buried deep inside. Chocolate-kiss encouragers are devoted and kind and know when to offer sympathetic words and actions. An encourager cherishes the opportunity to care.

QUIET ENCOURAGEMENT—LIKE A CHOCOLATE-KISS HUG

A hug is a kind of encouragement that doesn't make even a sound. In the fourth grade, I attended a small school—so small that the fourth and fifth grades were in the same room. In the fourth-grade group, I often passed out papers, cleaned the blackboards, and ran errands for the teacher. In the fifth-grade group, another girl, Lena, helped the teacher in the same way.

One afternoon on the playground, Lena called from atop her perch on the merry-go-round: "Here comes the teacher's pet." Never one to be outdone, I called back: "*You're* the real teacher's pet!"

Soon Lena and I were in a full-fledged, rolling, tumbling, hair-pulling fight. By the time the other kids pulled us apart, we were each a dirty, torn, and bloody mess. The teacher made us stand in front of the class the rest of the day and look each other in the eye. Humiliating. But I worried most about going home. I knew my big brother would tell Mother about the fight. My mom is a kind and gentle person, but she expected us to

> Chocolate is an antidepressant, which is especially useful as you start to gain weight.
>
> —JASON LOVE

behave; when we were wrong we were corrected. I expected (and deserved) punishment when I got home.

When I walked in the door, Mother never even mentioned the fight or my torn, dirty clothes. She helped me bathe my wounds and change into another outfit. She read to me and sang to me until I fell asleep. To this day, we've never discussed that fight.

> If not for chocolate, there would be no need for control-top pantyhose. An entire garment industry would be devastated.
>
> —AUTHOR UNKNOWN

Her kindness and loving care encouraged me to become a better person and to find other ways (better than name-calling and hair-pulling) to express myself.

She hugged me with her arms and her actions like a chocolate Hug. "Hugs" are chocolate kisses made of intertwined dark and white chocolate; they remind me that true friends sometimes respond with hugs.

In an article called "The Relationship Two-Step," Martha Beck wrote about how our body language causes us to respond. "A friend's shoulders slump half an inch, and without thinking we pat it encouragingly."[4] Friends encourage each other with smiles and pats on the shoulder.

COMMUNICATE ENCOURAGEMENT

Have you seen the bags of chocolate kisses wrapped in bright green and red foil at Christmastime? The brilliant colors announce the coming season joyfully. When we make a show of encouragement by speaking kind words, sending thoughtful cards and letters, and visiting in person, we are like sparkling, foiled-wrapped chocolate kisses.

The church council in Jerusalem sent Paul and Barnabas, along with Barsabbas and Silas, to Antioch. They sent a letter to the believers there, and "the people read it and were glad for its encouraging message."[5]

Imagine living in remote, evil Antioch and receiving a letter from the church leaders in Jerusalem. If the leaders took time to write, it must mean they cared. The letter tells how the Word of God spread around the world and explained to the believers in Antioch many of the truths about Jesus. Not only that, but the leaders in Jerusalem also sent the top guys to Antioch including Barsabbas and Silas, who "said much to encourage and strengthen the brothers."[6] Who wouldn't be encouraged by that!

An old story about a man falling into a well helps us understand the importance of encouragement. The man cried out for someone to help him. Soon a person came along and looked down into the well. The man in the well was relieved; someone had come to rescue him. A moment later, a folded piece of paper floated down. On the paper was a numbered list: "Ten Ways to Avoid Falling Into Wells."

When we are in deep trouble, we don't need censure or disapproval; we need a friend with a rope who will encourage us and rescue us.

When I first began speaking, a Christian educators' club invited me to make a presentation at their next meeting. The thought of standing in front of a bunch of schoolteachers intimidated and terrified me. I prepared my remarks weeks in advance, but as the date got closer, I doubted I could pull it off. One week before the big night, I found a card taped to my front door. The card encouraged me to rely on God. The next day, another card appeared. For seven days, I found a new card taped to the door every afternoon. Each card covered me with sweet encouragement. I used the last card in my closing remarks.

> Among life's mysteries is how a two-pound box of chocolate can make a woman five pounds heavier.
> —AUTHOR UNKNOWN

My friend Mary Sinclair placed those cards on my door because she believed I could do it. She went to so much effort that by the time of the event, I believed it myself. Her chocolate-kiss encouragement came in the form of a week's worth of encouragement cards. When I felt insecure, Mary encouraged me to take my first steps into the unknown world of public speaking.

SPEAK PEACE

The Bible says, "God made peace between us and himself, and God gave us the work of telling everyone about the peace we can have with him."[7]

To encourage others, we must learn to speak peace in the

middle of storms. Not a superficial "it'll be okay soon" kind of peace. Not a temporary truce, but true peace, initiated by God because He wants to be reconciled with us. The Father sent Jesus to the earth to implement His peace plan. Our job, as encouragers, is to tell others about the peace.

The peace of Jesus calms storms as He did on the Sea of Galilee. He said, "Peace, be still"[8] to the raging waters. He speaks peace to our storms too.

The peace of Jesus promotes confidence. Like the Roman centurion said, "Just say the word, and my servant will be healed."[9]

The peace of Jesus permeates every area of our lives. Like the fragrance that filled the air when Mary broke the alabaster box of perfume, Jesus's peace is a sweet aroma amid the smelly mess of life.

Jesus's peace occupied His hours on the cross. Though the weight of the world's sin tortured Him, He spoke peace. Jesus's peace can handle your worst nightmare too. Paul said, "He gave us this peace and we are sent to speak peace for Christ."[10]

When one of your girlfriends is overwhelmed with discouragement, bring her the chocolate of encouragement and peace.

ENCOURAGEMENT RENEWED

Picture a bathtub—empty, cold porcelain. Now, in your mind, turn on the faucet and adjust the temperature of the water to your liking. Now pour in some sweet-scented bubble bath. Suddenly the ordinary becomes extraordinary.

Out of one tablespoon of liquid comes a mountain of bubbles. The stronger the force of the water, the more bubbles. Armed with a few rich, dark-chocolate kisses, you can hardly wait to sink into the soothing pleasure of the filled tub.

But what happens if the phone rings? You have to shut off the faucet and go answer it. When you return, much of the fluff and fun may have disappeared.

Don't despair. You still have your bag of chocolates; all you have to do is turn the water on again—full force. What happens? Fresh bubbles appear. The tepid bathwater grows warm again. You have revived what seemed to be dying.

Now consider a girlfriend who needs you. The stronger you encourage her, the more she will bubble. Being an encourager requires you to be interested in others and to like even unlikable people. It requires that you ask God to help you be like Him.

The Bible says, "See to it, brothers, that none of you has a sinful, unbelieving heart that turns away from the living God. But encourage one another daily."[11]

UNEXPECTED BENEFIT

Paul encouraged the Roman church. He prayed for them. He yearned for them. He wrote, "I long to see you so that I may impart to you some spiritual gift to make you strong—that is, that you and I may be mutually encouraged by each other's faith."[12] He wanted them to grow stronger. He wanted to share his knowledge and his insight with them.

But Paul also knew that when he visited them, they would encourage him back. He wrote, "But don't think I'm not expecting to get something out of this, too! You have as much to give me as I do to you."[13] That's mutual encouragement.

So be encouraged, for there is much to hope for. And don't hesitate to be an encourager. What you say and how you live can make all the difference to another.

Bringing the Chocolate

1. Who has been an encourager in your life? Think of a specific time when he or she encouraged you. Describe that time in your journal, then write an encouraging note to that person.
2. In your own words, define *encouragement.*
3. Look up the word *encourage* in a Bible concordance and read as many verses as you can find that contain it. Write a short essay describing what you have learned.
4. Choose three people whose paths you cross regularly. Wrap up a box of chocolate kisses for each one and send them in the mail. Now make a list of two more ways you can encourage each one—and do it.

Prayer
Dear Lord, help me offer encouragement kisses
to those I meet today.

Offering Chocolate to My Friend

Dear friend, I'll give you encouragement to be all that God
wants you to be. If you think about quitting, call me instead.

Kiss-Kiss Bon-Bons

Ingredients:

2 cups all-purpose flour

1/2 cup chopped pecans

1 bag (12 oz.) semisweet chocolate chips

1/4 cup (1/2 stick) unsalted butter

1 14-oz. can sweetened condensed milk

1 teaspoon pure vanilla extract

1 package Hershey's Kisses, unwrapped

4 oz. white almond bark

Directions:

Preheat oven to 350°F.

In a large bowl, combine flour and pecans; set aside. In
another microwave-safe bowl, melt chocolate chips and butter;
stir until the mixture is smooth. Fold in the sweetened condensed
milk and vanilla and stir until well blended.

Add the melted chocolate mixture to the flour-and-pecan
mixture and blend well. Roll dough into one-inch balls, then

flatten in palm. Place a chocolate kiss on each flattened circle and enclose completely in the dough. Place on ungreased cookie sheets about one inch apart and bake until the tops begin to crack, approximately seven minutes. Transfer to wire racks to cool.

Topping: Melt white almond bark in a microwave-safe bowl and drizzle decoratively over the cookies.

Warm Chocolate-Chip-Cookie Sharing

Friendship is the comfort that comes from knowing that
even when you feel all alone, you aren't.
AUTHOR UNKNOWN

If you see some brother or sister in need and have the
means to do something about it but turn a cold shoulder
and do nothing, what happens to God's love? It
disappears. And you made it disappear.
1 JOHN 3:17, MSG

When I make chocolate-chip cookies, I double the amount of chocolate chips that the recipe calls for. In my opinion, the fun and flavor of a chocolate-chip cookie comes from the sweet, creamy, yummy chip, and that extra quantity of chocolate multiplies the fun.

Like a chocolate-chip cookie without chocolate chips, friendship without sharing is uninteresting, lackluster, and tedious. Only friends who are willing to maximize effort and pour double energy into the friendship are unforgettable friends, because true friendship, the chocolate-chip-cookie-sharing kind, requires giving the full measure of oneself. It means big expenditures of time, emotions, and even money.

My husband, George, considers himself a chocolate-chip cookie connoisseur. He thinks he can tell if a chocolate-chip cookie is homemade in one bite. Testing his skill has become a family contest. Sometimes when I'm in a hurry I'll make chocolate-chip cookies from a boxed mix. But he always knows that the batter wasn't mixed from scratch. Frozen cookie dough tastes remarkably like homemade to me; in fact, I can't tell the difference. When I first discovered this product, I couldn't wait to try it on George. I baked a batch for him and sat him down at the table with a warm cookie and the mandatory glass of cold milk. I could see the chocolate chips melting as he took his first bite. He closed his eyes while he chewed and made an *Mmmm* sound. He smiled.

I have him, I thought.

Then he said, "Close, but not the real thing."

Something about the sugar content or the crispiness of the mix or frozen dough doesn't quite replicate the original. George likes cookies made from fresh ingredients put together with my personal touch.

It is really easy to break off those squares of the frozen cookie dough and place them on a cookie sheet. The cookies always turn out flawless. I think they are great, but to thoroughly please George, I have to put in the extra time and effort and make the cookies from scratch.

BIG SPENDER

Friendships are like that. To share in our girlfriend's world or to fully know and appreciate her, we must become "big spenders." We need to be willing to expend time and emotions for our friend. We also need to be willing to splurge on her, if necessary, in order to share chocolate-chip friendship. And in the spending, we spenders find unexpected joy—like a cookie with double chips in every bite.

Every month I invite a group of writer friends to my home to critique each other's work and to lavish encouragement on each other. I cook a meal. All the participants say, "You don't have to cook for us; we'd come anyway." But I love to cook, I love these writer friends, and cooking is my opportunity to serve them. It's a wonderful combination of great food, pretty dishes, and good friends.

Katie is in her twenties, while the rest of us…well, let's just say that the rest of us are not. Katie loves us and never misses a meeting. She enjoys the camaraderie the group is built on when we meet together to share a common love—writing.

But Katie doesn't want to eat. I don't know why. Maybe she

doesn't like the food, or maybe she is already full. However, Katie loves warm chocolate-chip cookies with big chunks of chocolate and no nuts. So even if I prepare a dessert recipe for the group, I always bake a batch of chocolate-chip cookies and have a jug of milk in the fridge ready for Katie. It's my way of telling her that I love her, that she's special to me, and that I'm glad she came.

Time and effort spent on a friend doesn't have to be over-whelming or expensive. Chocolate-chip-sharing friendship means opening my heart and hands to my friend.

> If you've got melted chocolate all over your hands, you are eating it too slowly.
> —AUTHOR UNKNOWN

The correlation between sharing warm cookies and sharing true friend-ship stuns me. No matter how im-perfect my friendship is, if I am willing to share myself with another girlfriend, she will respond. The effort of making cook-ies always makes those around me smile, just as the effort of offer-ing friendship to another person always results in unforgettable moments of joy.

According to the Bible, it is not real friendship if we just talk about it. "My dear children, let's not just talk about love; let's practice real love. This is the only way we'll know we're living truly, living in God's reality."[1] Practicing love is more than saying the words. It's more than tributes or even gifts. Practicing real love requires every part of your life to be filled with the sweet grace of giving—like a chocolate-chip cookie with double the chips.

RING AND RUN GANG

Late one night as George and I sat reading in our recliners, the doorbell rang. George got up and went to the front door, only to find no one there. Then he looked down. There on our porch was a platter covered in plastic wrap. We had been the victims of a ring-and-run gang who chose us as the recipient of a delicious plate of chocolate-chip cookies.

I never found out which of my friends left the cookies (I have narrowed it to two), but I knew somewhere out there a girlfriend loved me enough to take the time and effort to drop off a plate of cookies. I felt loved and encouraged. Someone had planned a way to surprise and delight me.

The Bible says, "Just as lotions and fragrance give sensual delight, a sweet friendship refreshes the soul."[2] Even if it's a little outrageous, the unexpected surprise of finding out someone thought of you is just one of the ways friendship refreshes and builds joy.

TIME MATTERS

Our doorbell rang again one night around nine. There stood our friends Steve, Joni, Bruce, and Connie. The foursome had decided we should be with them, so they came to pick us up unannounced. Eager for friendship, we climbed into their SUV and drove around picking up other couples for a fun evening together.

The focus and concentration they put on spending time together showed a love and commitment that has developed into a lifelong friendship. The fun we had that evening meant more than sermons, lectures, or platitudes about friendship ever would.

Some months later this same little band left a huge plastic lion on our lawn. When we found it the next morning, we immediately began plotting which of our friends should be the next recipient of the giant feline.

Time spent on friendship matters. The fact that our friends spent time thinking of ways to share their lives (and plastic lions) with us meant a lot. Just as chocolate-chip cookies with no chips are not good, friendship without the investment of time can be boring, lackluster, and uninteresting.

A Friend Who Doesn't Judge

Friendship not only takes time and creativity; it also flourishes when friends are willing to accept failures and foibles in each other.

The apostle Paul discusses the importance of not judging others in Romans 14. Instead of complaining about what other people eat or don't eat or how they worship, we are to let people live as they are convinced to live. It is not our job to judge. It is our job to love. Let people be accountable to God. If we judge

too sternly, we become an obstacle to a friend who may be struggling with faith or life purpose.

On the other hand, we need to be mindful of what we do. If
I eat or drink something or act in a way my friend thinks is
wrong, I hurt her. True friendship decides not to participate in
any activity that would cause a friend to stumble, because "the
kingdom of God is not a matter of eating and drinking, but of
righteousness, peace and joy."[3]

By understanding the principles Paul lays out in Romans 14,
we see that it is up to us to keep friendships intact. It is our job
not to cause trouble, and to avoid anything that could conceiv-
ably carry even the tiniest inkling of a chance to harm a friend.
As Paul puts it, "Make every effort to do what leads to peace and
to mutual edification."[4]

WE NEED EACH OTHER

In the 1600s, the poet John Donne wrote a meditation that uses
the metaphor of landmass to express how much friendship is necessary to us. He wrote, "No man is an island, entire of itself.
Every man is a piece of the continent, a part of the main."[5]

Without friendship, I am like a broken cookie: still me, but
missing an important part. Incomplete. In today's cell phone-
crazed culture, everywhere you go you see dozens of people on
the phone. It seems we can't go to the mall, shop at a store, take

in a ball game, visit a doctor's office, drive on the freeway, or sit at an office desk without checking in with friends. We synchronize our schedules and plan our next time to meet. Satellite technology keeps us connected.

I'm not saying that cell phones are always good for friendship. My friend and daughter-in-law, Kathryn, reminds me that cell phones also disconnect us: picture two girlfriends meeting for lunch, neither able to complete a sentence because their cells phones keep ringing. The very thing meant to connect instead distracts us.

Time spent together *without interruptions* produces spiritual friendships. Let satellite technology keep us connected, but never make it a substitute for real, face-to-face connections.

We aren't in isolation. We need to connect. *We need each other.*

NOT ME BUT YOU

Friendship requires sacrifice. Developing true, rich, deep friendship—the chocolate-chip-cookie-sharing kind—is hard work. It takes effort, concentration, and planning. And it costs us emotionally, too.

When He was thirty years old, Jesus began walking through the region called Galilee, choosing His disciples along the way. He saw some fishermen and asked them to follow Him. He saw some businessmen and said, "Come with me." Twelve of these followers became the disciples who traveled with Jesus for the next three years. They listened to His teaching, watched Him perform miracles, and observed how much He loved the people in the towns and cities they visited.

Some of these disciples left homes and abandoned businesses. Others left fathers, mothers, brothers, and sisters. Some traveled far away from wives and children. I'm sure they loved their families and their homes and probably worried about what would happen while they were gone. Peter once said to Jesus, "We have left everything to follow you."[6] Why did they forfeit everything?

> When the going gets tough, the tough eat chocolate.
> —AUTHOR UNKNOWN

They followed Jesus because they wanted to know God. Each of them gave up possessions and comforts to join the itinerant ministry of the One they believed was the Messiah. They were seeking truth. They recognized Jesus as the Master Teacher, and they pursued Him.

After three years, an amazing thing happened. Just before Jesus went to the cross, He said, "I'm no longer calling you servants because servants don't understand what their master is thinking and planning. No, I've named you friends because I've let you in on everything I've heard from the Father."[7]

These disciples put life on hold to follow Jesus and received an incomparable bonus: deep, intimate friendship with the Master. These servants became friends when each changed his focus from self to Christ.

True friendship is voluntary willingness to sacrifice yourself for the friendship. You can hardly impose or presume on an intimate friend. Cherished friends do not keep score about whose turn it is. Dear friends are unselfish and care more for each other than for themselves.

For me, opening myself to someone else often feels unnatural. Sacrificing physically is much easier. I can "do" things for people over and over because of my choleric work-first-and-foremost personality. I am always busy doing, but I rarely let anyone in on my inner feelings. Becoming a chocolate-chip kind of friend requires me to open up.

Extra Effort

During my childhood, Daddy made an annual trip to north central Texas to buy bushels of sweet, juicy peaches, which Mama carefully peeled and sliced. After covering the peaches in thick, sugary syrup, she sealed them in plastic bags and transferred the bags to our big chest freezer.

As a little girl, I struggled to lift the heavy door of the freezer a few inches so that I could squeeze my arm in, reach down, and get one of the frozen packages. Too impatient to wait for thawing (this was before microwaves), I would chop, tug, and pry at those peaches with a fork until finally a frozen morsel popped loose. Those sweet, cold peaches were incredibly delicious. Often my brother and I would each eat a whole package in one afternoon.

One day my husband and I were driving along a highway when we saw a sign: Fresh Peaches for Sale. We stopped, bought a bushel, and took them home. I planned to make the same peaches for my kids that Mother made. *Surely they would rise up and call me blessed.*

> Like love, chocolate is always a delight to receive or to give.
> —MARY JANE FINSAND,
> THE DIABETIC CHOCOLATE
> COOKBOOK

I stood at the kitchen sink, the basket of plump red-and-gold spheres on the counter beside me, softly singing to myself as I worked the paring knife under the fuzzy skin of the ripe peach. A proud feeling swelled inside me.

"What a wonderful memory," I said aloud. "My children will reminisce about this someday." I continued peeling and slicing, feeling smug.

Before long, however, my mood changed. *Why doesn't that mountain of peaches seem to get any smaller?* I wondered. *I'm beginning to hate peaches. How long have I been at this job?*

I stretched my neck and rolled my shoulders. *I don't remember Mother ever mentioning that her back hurt from standing so long at the sink, peeling these things.*

I stopped, dialed Mother's number, and almost shouted,

"Mother, why didn't you tell me that peeling peaches was such hard work? I'm sure not going to let my kids just eat them for snacks anytime they feel like it." When I was through with my tirade, I asked, "Why did you let us do that? Did you know that each one of us ate whole packages by ourselves? I'm going to save my peaches for someone special!"

She answered, "I *did* make them for someone special. You and your brother."

Okay, I know it isn't a story about chocolate, but my peach story does give us a glimpse of what it means to give unselfishly and even go through some pain to share with someone else.

Like me as a child eating frozen peaches without understanding the sacrifice that had gone into them, our friends won't always know how much effort we put into the friendship. But *we'll* know. The true joy of sharing is like my mother's joy in watching us eat her peaches.

Las cosas claras y el chocolate espeso.
(Ideas should be clear, and chocolate thick.)
—SPANISH PROVERB

Friendship is about considering others more than yourself. Friendship is not being too tired or too busy to listen to a friend's story. Friendship is patience when friends make bad decisions or poor choices. Friendship is spending whatever we have—energy, emotions, money, patience—and sometimes doing a little unpleasant work for others. Only then will we develop intimate, chocolate-chip-cookie-sharing friends.

The phrase "If there's anything I can do, just let me know"

won't suffice in a time of crisis. People don't know what they need when they are in a crisis. Don't disappear on your friend. Figure out something to do.

My friend Joy Simpson lost her beautiful, talented daughter in a car accident. We went to her home immediately to offer our love to Joy and David. The house was filled with friends bearing food and hugs and sharing tears. As the days and weeks passed, some friends kept coming but others disappeared.

The friends that really helped Joy and David were the ones who continued to come over and those who called in the weeks and months following the tragedy. Girlfriends who encouraged Joy to talk about her grief and to tell stories about Brittany. Friends who helped occupy the hours of spring break when their daughter would have been home visiting from college. Couples who remembered the anniversary of Brittany's death.

Remember, helping a friend is a marathon, not a sprint. You must seek your friend's company even if you don't know what to say or do. Just being there makes a difference.

It's Not Easy

Being a chocolate-chip friend isn't easy. As the old saying goes, some people make enemies instead of friends because it's less trouble.

But you really haven't lived until you have done something for someone who cannot make your life better. Sacrificed for someone who cannot repay the favor. Jesus is the ultimate example of this kind of sacrifice. He came to earth from heaven just to give us life.

> If you have any encouragement from being united with
> Christ, if any comfort from his love, if any fellowship
> with the Spirit, if any tenderness and compassion, then
> make my joy complete by being like-minded, having the
> same love, being one in spirit and purpose. Do nothing
> out of selfish ambition or vain conceit, but in humility
> consider others better than yourselves. Each of you should
> look not only to your own interests, but also to the
> interests of others.
>
> Your attitude should be the same as that of Christ
> Jesus: Who, being in very nature God, did not consider
> equality with God something to be grasped, but made
> himself nothing, taking the very nature of a servant, being
> made in human likeness. And being found in appearance
> as a man, he humbled himself and became obedient to
> death—even death on a cross![8]

Imagine Jesus, sitting on His throne in heaven. It can't get much better than that! Yet He came to earth, made Himself nothing, took the nature of a servant, became a human, and obeyed God so completely that He even endured the cross, dying voluntarily on our behalf. His sacrifice wasn't easy, but He did it for us. He became broken bread and poured-out wine for us, His enemies at the time.

While in our sin, we are separated from Him; yet He loved us enough to give His all. When we accepted His gift, we became His friends. Real friendship does the same for others.

Sharing Great Chunks of Chocolate

Lately I've been noticing chocolate-chip cookies that have big chunks of chocolate instead of simple little chips. I am stunned when I eat one of these luscious things. The chocolate overwhelms each bite. To qualify for this kind of chocolate-chip-cookie-sharing friendship, we must infuse our friendships with unexpected, over-the-top sharing.

Touching someone who is in pain is the ultimate friendship. Those precious moments when you hug a friend or hold her hand or touch her arm are vital. And when your friend's circumstance is dire, your willingness to help with private necessities of life is the rich sharing that can only come from a friend who is full of giant chocolate chips.

An Unexpected Friend

A chocolate-chip cookie with white chocolate chips surprises the taste buds. In the same way, sometimes someone you never thought would become a friend grows into a lifeline to the future.

That's what happened to four thirty-something girls who became unexpected girlfriends when they met for the first time, ten months after 9/11. "Lunch with 'the girls,' as they call themselves, begins with their traditional glass-clinking, hearty toast: 'To the boys.'"[9]

"The boys" were their husbands. All were killed in the World Trade Center collapse. None of these women knew each other before the tragedy, but now they are part of a club no one wanted to join. Unexpectedly thrown together through tragic circumstances, these widows share the worst of grief and the best of friendship.

> I have this theory that chocolate slows down the aging process.... It may not be true, but do I dare take the chance?
> —AUTHOR UNKNOWN

They celebrate their lives before 9/11 and the pain and awkwardness following. The friendship has chronicled everything from the rites of widowhood (taking off wedding rings, removing a husband's outgoing message on the answering machine) to their future hopes. They love, laugh, share, and cry together. They have even coauthored a book.

These four friends don't have to ask the probing questions that outsiders ask. Each one knows how the others are feeling and functioning. Forging this unexpected friendship has replaced despair with optimism.

None of them has a political or economic agenda. The group itself fulfills each one's need for friendship. Their book title is taken from an offhand comment one of them made during a vacation together: *Love You, Mean It.* The phrase has become the trademark way to end e-mails to each other, shortened to LUMI. As Julia Collins, one of the women in the group, says, "The message is clear. Love is a gift. Share it."[10]

Friendship is made for sharing. I give you a part of me, and you give me a part of you. As we deal with crisis events in our lives, we share the pain and the recovery. Just like double chocolate chips in a cookie, you can never get enough of a friend who is willing to share.

Bringing the Chocolate

1. Describe what happened when a friend shared her life with you in a generous, unexpected way.
2. How much are you willing to spend—mentally, emotionally, financially—on your newest friend?
3. Think of a plan to surprise a friend involving chocolate-chip cookies. Write the plan here (and don't forget to double the chips in your recipe).
4. What life event or circumstances brought a special friend into your world (for example, having a baby, suffering a tragedy, moving to a new city)? Describe how your special friend helped you.

Prayer
Dear Lord, rebuild my heart into a sharing heart,
ready to give all I have to my friend.

Offering Chocolate to My Friend
Dear friend, I'll give you myself
even when it is inconvenient for me.

Yes, George, These Are Homemade Buffalo Chips

Blend:

2 cups (4 sticks) unsalted butter, melted

2 cups brown sugar

2 cups granulated sugar

Stir in:

4 large eggs

2 teaspoons pure vanilla extract

Sift together, then add:

4 cups flour

2 teaspoons baking powder

2 teaspoons baking soda

1 teaspoon salt

Fold in thoroughly:

2 cups old-fashioned oatmeal

1 bag (12 oz.) semisweet chocolate chips

1 cup chopped pecans

2 cups flaked sweetened coconut

Directions:

Preheat the oven to 350°F.

Use an ice cream scoop to portion dough onto a greased cookie sheet, placing only six cookies on each cookie sheet. Make a slight indention in the back of each ball with the ice-cream scoop, then transfer to the oven and bake for about fifteen minutes. Cool before removing to wire racks.

Note: This makes a big batch of big cookies!

A Godiva Kind of Forgiveness

There is nothing better than a good friend,
except a good friend with chocolate.
LINDA GRAYSON IN *THE PICKWICK PAPERS*
BY CHARLES DICKENS

Finally, all of you, live in harmony with one another; be
sympathetic, love as brothers, be compassionate and
humble. Do not repay evil with evil or insult with insult,
but with blessing, because to this you were called
so that you may inherit a blessing.
1 PETER 3:8–9

Elizabeth told me about her broken friendship with Glenda. "I never felt closer to a girlfriend than I did to Glenda. She understood me, and I understood her. If she saw me across a crowded room, she knew immediately if something was amiss in my life.

"I don't know how she developed this intuitive quality, but I came to count on it. We often laughed because she saw through my coordinated clothes and shoes and practiced smile to my impatience and frustration—something even my own husband couldn't see. I treasured her whispered encouragement and those long, open-your-heart-and-let-it-all-hang-out talks.

"But one evening she came to my house to complain about my son's behavior. What she said about him proved mostly true and he certainly needed correction, but the shock that disintegrated our friendship was that her criticisms were not cloaked in love. Her words weren't constructive criticism. She gave up on him and crossed him off her list. She condemned him and saw no future for him. In her mind he had failed, and there could be no redemption. At least that's how she made me feel.

"My son was seventeen and finding his way in the big, scary world of young adulthood. He was enamored with a girlfriend and overflowing with hormones. She had seen them together in an inappropriate place. I wasn't happy with the choices he made but hoped he would change. She threw hope, and him, in the trash bin. After she left that night, I never heard from her again."

Elizabeth wrote in her journal:

Oh, my friend. I miss you. Yet I am so angry.
Why are you willing to throw William away?
What do you really expect of him? He's my son,
for crying out loud!

For crying out loud. That's how I feel. I am
crying out loud for you. I need you to help me
through this, not condemn him and me with him.
Please don't turn your back on me.

Elizabeth's friendship with Glenda disappeared because of bad feelings, misplaced words, and misunderstandings. Elizabeth changed churches and made new acquaintances, but the loss of this friendship impacted her ability to find or trust a new best friend.

Carrying around the pain of betrayal isn't easy to recognize in ourselves, but when we come face to face with it, we have to choose whether to forgive or not.

BUT I DON'T WANT TO FORGIVE

Our little group of four met every week to cling to each other's faith, hoping to ease our pain. A friend of ours, a church youth leader, had plunged into unspeakable sin. We watched our teenagers grapple with hurt and disappointment. And we were angry. We felt we could never forgive. She deserved to be punished, and we hoped she felt miserable.

At our meetings, we worked our way through the book of Jonah. Watching God intervene in the reluctant prophet's life. When we came to the last chapter, we mocked poor Jonah a bit.

Sitting out there on the hill. Whining. Pouting. Then someone said, "Jonah's big problem was that he didn't want to forgive those Ninevites."

I suddenly saw myself on that hillside sitting beside Jonah, and I heard God's quiet nudge. "You won't forgive either, will you?"[1]

God was right. I enjoyed harboring bad feelings toward my former friend. Smug and virtuous, I stewed over the terrible injuries she had inflicted.

God must have guffawed at my righteous indignation. It *was* comical, considering my own penchant for failure and sin. But at that moment I was too wrapped up in my contempt for her. I dreamed of ways that God would "get" her. I saw her waking up early one morning and saying, "Oh no, what have I done?" I visualized opening my front door to find her standing there in disheveled confusion, crying for forgiveness. I saw her tired, alone, sad, and having a bad-hair day.

GENUINE GODIVA-LIKE FORGIVENESS

Why is it that we consider some sins so much worse than others? We love to rank everyone else's sin and then raise high our self-righteous Olympic scorecards. We speak of our own sin in amiable tones and give it names like *oversight, blunder,* or *faux pas* (as if calling sin by a French name will make it more palatable).

But when others sin, we name it Sin with a capital S and pronounce it using a Texas drawl (in three syllables).

When a friend's sin has directly affected us or hurt someone we love, we allow the pain and the shame to swallow us up in its forceful grip. We relive the misery in our waking hours and dream never-ending revenge dreams in our sleep. Even when we try to push the pain away, it develops a life of its own, worming its way into our minds at the most inconvenient times.

Our self-love gets in the way. We've been hurt. We are angry. We deserve an apology. Like Jonah, we are pouting and mad. What a waste of our time, emotions, mental capacities, spiritual vitality, and potential.

Forgiving others who have hurt us is tricky and demanding. The Bible says, "Do not repay evil with evil or insult with insult, but with blessing."[2] Though we might crave retribution and revenge, we can only discover true forgiveness by showering blessings, rich as Godiva

> What is the meaning of life? All evidence to date suggests that it's chocolate.
> —AUTHOR UNKNOWN

chocolate, on someone who has hurt us. I can release the offender by praying blessings on her.

True forgiveness is not trying to forget the offense; rather, it is a willingness and desire for *God to bless the offender*. When we can say, "God bless her," we have opened a new world of possibilities—like lifting the golden lid on a box of Godiva chocolates.

When we pray for God to shower blessings, opportunities for ministry, and love from all kinds of people, we forgive.

As long as I focus on me and my pain, I will never be able to focus on a future that includes a life of joy, happiness, and ministry for me or for her. Unless I can look into the future and see her as still qualified to serve God in some way (even after what she did to me), I haven't truly forgiven.

Godiva chocolate can't be successfully replicated; the recipes are exclusive and unattainable, the chocolate combinations unique to the company. Any copy would lack the authenticity of a real box of the sweet concoctions. Forgiveness must be genuine too. Genuine enough that when we are offended, we will ultimately be able to forgive enough to ask God to bless the offender.

THE SOURCE OF FORGIVENESS

There is nothing inside us that will make us magnanimous enough to forgive a friend who has wronged us. We don't have that capacity; it's not in our nature. But when we develop the nature of Christ, He begins to infuse our inability with His ability. When our hearts change, our perspective changes.

David the psalmist spoke often about the remarkable forgiveness of God. David committed a lot of big sins, some we shudder to think about, yet he received God's forgiveness. Even when David felt his sin was too great to be forgiven, he said, "When we were overwhelmed by sins, you forgave our transgressions."[3]

Israel broke God's heart because the people He loved so much turned away from Him again and again. "Yet he was merciful; he forgave their iniquities and did not destroy them. Time after time he restrained his anger and did not stir up his full wrath. He remembered that they were but flesh, a passing breeze that does not return."[4]

In the Old Testament, the message of God's continual forgiveness and hope for Israel shines through every book. He remembered that they were human and prone to mistakes. In the same way, Godiva forgiveness recognizes that our friends are flawed human beings.

> In the beginning, the Lord created chocolate, and He saw that it was good. Then He separated the light from the dark and it was better.
> —AUTHOR UNKNOWN

Jesus put enormous emphasis on human-to-human forgiveness. When Peter questioned about forgiveness, Jesus opened the door for new thinking. "Then Peter came to Jesus and asked, 'Lord, how many times shall I forgive my brother when he sins against me? Up to seven times?' Jesus answered, 'I tell you, not seven times, but seventy-seven times.'"[5]

According to Jesus, we should never quit forgiving. He illustrated that point with a story.

Therefore, the kingdom of heaven is like a king who wanted to settle accounts with his servants. As he began the settlement, a man who owed him ten thousand talents was brought to him. Since he was not able to pay, the master ordered that he and his wife and his children and all that he had be sold to repay the debt.

The servant fell on his knees before him. "Be patient with me," he begged, "and I will pay back everything." The servant's master took pity on him, canceled the debt and let him go.

But when that servant went out, he found one of his fellow servants who owed him a hundred denarii. He grabbed him and began to choke him. "Pay back what you owe me!" he demanded.

His fellow servant fell to his knees and begged him, "Be patient with me, and I will pay you back."

But he refused. Instead, he went off and had the man thrown into prison until he could pay the debt. When the other servants saw what had happened, they were greatly distressed and went and told their master everything that had happened.

Then the master called the servant in. "You wicked servant," he said, "I canceled all that debt of yours because you begged me to. Shouldn't you have had mercy on your fellow servant just as I had on you?" In anger his master turned him over to the jailers to be tortured, until he should pay back all he owed.

This is how my heavenly Father will treat each of you unless you forgive your brother from your heart.[6]

In this parable about the unforgiving servant, Jesus commands us to forgive because we have been forgiven. For believers, forgiveness is our great legacy from Christ. We pass the legacy along when we forgive our friends.

RICH AS GODIVA

Godiva chocolates come in a special gold box that is highly recognizable, expensive, and exclusive. Forgiveness is like that gold box; although it is not easily obtainable, it is the bright reward for following God's plan.

In his letter to the Christ followers who lived at Corinth, Paul asked each one to forgive for the sake of the person who was wrong. "Now instead, you ought to forgive and comfort him, so that he will not be overwhelmed by excessive sorrow. I urge you, therefore, to reaffirm your love for him."[7] Forgiveness is the fundamental condition for friendship.

Paul gave us further instructions in his letter to the Colossian church. "Bear with each other and forgive whatever grievances you may have against one another. Forgive as the Lord forgave you. And over all these virtues put on love, which binds them all together in perfect unity."[8]

Only God can pull me from the black hole of anger and show me that by forgiving I will help the other person. Even further, only God can change my heart and mind and make me even want to help that other person. Real forgiveness comes only when I release the person who hurt me.

Now might be a good time to stop and pray a simple prayer for someone who has hurt you. It isn't easy, but don't resist this opportunity to start the healing journey by choosing right now to begin the process of forgiving. Say a prayer like this: "Lord, I don't want to forgive her because she hurt me, but after reading these paragraphs, I realize that I am holding on to a lot of anger. I ask You to replace my anger and hurt with forgiveness. I ask You to help me release her to You. Fill me with the desire to see her totally restored to You and fully engaged in ministry again. I don't have the strength to forgive and bless her on my own, but You can fill me with Your grace. Lord, please give her wonderful opportunities to serve You, and bless her with a joy-filled life."

UNEXPECTED BENEFIT

Godiva is creamy and rich with flavor like no other sweet creation. I experience an unexpected euphoria when I savor each morsel and slowly let the flavor and fragrance wash over me. Forgiveness is like that—something happens that I never expected. In the process of forgiving, I become free.

It is a startling phenomenon. Freedom washes over you. Freedom from that nagging, gnawing irritation that wouldn't go away. Freedom from that urge to see her punished. Freedom from waiting to see what God is going to do to her for what she did.

Free, yes, free indeed. No longer stewing over her fate. No longer waiting for that moment of confrontation. (No more secretly practicing what I might say.) Only God can transform unforgiveness into freedom.

> Everyone has a price—mine is chocolate.
> —AUTHOR UNKNOWN

Forgiveness means that ugly rancor, loathing, bitterness, and hate don't control my thoughts anymore. I don't replay her words over and over. Thoughts of revenge don't interrupt my fun. I am free to enjoy the richness of life like a bite of a Godiva chocolate truffle.

Freedom is sweeter than the richest Godiva chocolate. Freedom is that ooey-gooey, drippy deliciousness that delights us when we wake each morning. When I have forgiven, I am unquestionably free.

JUST A LITTLE BIT

Successful forgiveness, I've found, is a lot like a meal cooked in a Crock-Pot, not a microwave. We can't decide at three in the afternoon to stop hating and start forgiving. It's not like making a sharp U-turn in the road or choosing a truffle from the Godiva box. It is a deliberate, calculated, step-by-step process. Movement by movement we decide, then take a tiny step. *Right now I'll do this to get me started in the direction of forgiveness.* Forgiving is consistent and persistent. Those two vital virtues only come through Jesus.

Noelle Quinn and Kari West wrote a book titled *When He Leaves*. Both authors experienced the pain of a husband's betrayal, followed by divorce. Noelle writes,

> There was a time when anger was the only justifiable response to what happened. I even ripped pictures of Dan out of the scrapbooks. The time came to move beyond, not because of what Dan said, but in spite of it. Forgiveness became a journey that is unhurried. At first I could only pray, "Lord, Dan doesn't deserve it and I don't feel like it, but I forgive him." Each day I pray to forgive at least one percent more, but I don't have to keep worrying about whether I've forgiven or not. I told Dan, "I am forgiving by degrees. I'm not there 100 percent but I'm on my way."[9]

Just as the best Godiva chocolates sometimes come two to a tiny box, a little bit of forgiveness is powerful and just 1 percent more can enrich your life.

CRITICAL INGREDIENT

Forgiveness is critical to true friendship. Forgiveness is like one of those Godiva chocolate pieces with the surprise filling. Forgiveness astonishes us with joy and freedom. Freedom allows us to push each other toward Jesus.

If I can learn to extend grace with every word I speak, I will taste the chocolate. If I can say something that will help a friend follow Jesus—even if she doesn't deserve the kindness—I will experience the rich flavor of a mended relationship.

Earlier I quoted Hebrews 10:24—"Let us consider how to stimulate one another to love and good deeds."[10] Forgiveness is a great foundation where we can build relationships and begin spurring each other on to greater things. When I pray blessing on someone who hurt me, steer her toward Jesus, and ask God to give her a new and fresh ministry, I have gathered the first ingredients for a rich-as-Godiva friendship.

NOT A FORMULA

I'm not fond of formulas for Christian living. "Ten steps to happiness" or "seven ways to finding true joy" always fall flat with me. It seems when I get to step number ten or way number seven, I am disappointed and discouraged because the formula didn't work and I haven't realized whatever success the plan promised.

But I have discovered that to restore friendship we must intentionally do whatever is necessary to forgive. Maybe some of the following practical ideas will point you in the direction of forgiveness. If they do, I hope you savor the success of forgiveness like sweet Godiva chocolate melting on your lips. Even if your friend doesn't respond, I know that sweet freedom will flow through your life.

UNDERSTANDING FORGIVENESS

When George and I speak at marriage retreats, we give participants the *A's* to understanding forgiveness by sharing with them what forgiveness is *not*: amnesia, acquittal, award, approval, or acquiescence.[11]

Forgiveness isn't *amnesia* so that we quit remembering the pain. It doesn't *acquit* the person or presume them blameless or excused. Forgiveness doesn't reward bad behavior or *approve* the thing they did. And forgiveness certainly doesn't *acquiesce*, meaning the offender can continue inflicting pain on us.

What forgiveness actually does is recognize its severity and *acknowledge* it. "Forgiveness is a response that seeks to redeem the hurt, not brush it off."[12]

I listened to a popular radio program recently where the speaker said you couldn't forgive someone until the person repented and asked for forgiveness. His premise was that we can't be more forgiving than God is and God forgives when we repent.

Although I would never presume to do what God does, I think that radio host is wrong. God forgives and washes away my sins completely, making me whole before Him. We can't possibly duplicate that amazing grace and mercy or power.

However, in our person-to-person relationships, we can forgive what others have done to us whether they repent or not. When we do forgive, we are not absolving them of sin; we are only taking away the barriers between us. If my forgiveness of another person is dependent on her willingness to admit that she is wrong, what if she never regrets what she did? Then I'm the one who harbors the pain.

> Above all...
> think chocolate!
> —BETTY CROCKER

How do I walk in that? How do I carry around the ugly, dark aversion in my heart? Where do I put the burden, the pain, and the icky feelings? It is far better to initiate the forgiveness; only then am I free. Only then are the murky blemishes of loathing cleared out of my soul.

God alone holds the guilty accountable. God alone is the judge who dishes out punishment. Yet He forgives us over and over again. We are not judges or executioners, but with God's help and the Spirit's leading, we can be forgivers.

God offers ultimate forgiveness to those who trust Him. We can model the forgiveness with our friends. He forgives us, we forgive others, and His mercy overflows from our life to theirs.

TALK TO GOD FIRST

Before you rush to that girlfriend who has hurt you and spill your pain on her, ask God for wisdom, discernment, and timing. Some situations do not require face-to-face confrontation. My friend Leeann, a pastor's wife, received a visit from a former church member who said, "I really hated you when you lived in our town, and I just wanted to tell you that I've forgiven you for everything."

Leeann never knew this woman harbored all these bad feelings or what brought on the need for forgiveness. Leeann's shock left her too stunned to even clarify what the woman meant. Like many of us would do, she stood there horrified, her mouth agape, and said, "Okay."

Later Leeann agonized. What had she done to the woman? What had she said? The woman went away happy and carefree because she had unloaded her pain, but she left a black cloud over Leeann.

In this situation (and maybe in yours), the woman should have dealt with her ill feelings alone and realized there was no specific incident to confront. If she talked to God first, He might have told her to settle it in her own heart and not inflict unnecessary pain into Leeann's life. Or perhaps God could have helped her speak in love and kindness. As it happened, the woman felt great and Leeann suffered. Not exactly Godiva freedom.

BE THE FIRST TO ACT

Although speaking directly to the person may not be the way to handle your problem, don't let the fact that you might not have a confrontation somehow trick you into never doing the hard work of forgiveness. You must settle the issue in your own heart no matter what the other person does.

Face to Face

While there are certain situations like Leeann's when it's not necessary to confront another person, most of the time a sincere willingness to apologize, forgive, and reconcile is best handled face to face.

> The Twelve-Step Program for Chocoholics: Never be more than twelve steps away from chocolate!
> —TERRY MOORE

Jesus said, "This is how I want you to conduct yourself in these matters. If you enter your place of worship and, about to make an offering, you suddenly remember a grudge a friend has against you, abandon your offering, leave immediately, go to this friend and make things right."[13]

In this instruction, He tells us to be proactive. Did you notice that He said "a grudge a friend has against you"? Not if you have a grudge against her. According to Jesus's directive, I am supposed to be the first to act if a friend holds something against me, whether real or imagined.

Be the forgiver and the reconciler. Sympathize with her feelings. Listen instead of accusing. Admit your part in the conflict. Do the work to discover the problem instead of blaming her. Disarm. Put down the weapons of sarcasm, derision, and ridicule. Ask God to make whatever changes are necessary in you so that your friendship can be restored.

After God confronted my Jonah-like attitude about my former friend, I wrote her a letter explaining about my study of the book of Jonah and how God used the Bible to stop my judgmental attitude. I told her my love was unconditional and my forgiveness was complete.

When She Won't Respond

If you forgive your friend and she doesn't respond, don't limit your own recovery because of her refusal. Forgiveness is not dependent on the other person. You can't change her. You are not responsible for her actions or for her happiness. Don't get sucked back into the hurt, the emotional debt, the need for revenge, and the rage. When you forgive, you move out of the bondage into celebration. It doesn't mean you forget; it means you choose not to react further.

Remember my friend Elizabeth? She chose to forgive. She called repeatedly, but Glenda screened the calls. Finally Elizabeth prayed. She asked God to mend the rips in her heart from what Glenda did and to soothe and comfort Glenda for the unkind things Elizabeth inflicted too—even if they never saw each other again.

Take Responsibility for What I Did

Author Judy Hampton wrote, "When I forgive the people who hurt me in the past, I have to take more responsibility for my present."[14]

When all you can think about is what awful things she did to you, you need a new perspective to see what awful things you did to her. To see where you are culpable. It is so easy to think only of your own pain, misery, unhappiness, and how *she* hurt you, and not realize how much you may have hurt her. There is no way out of this downward spiral of loathing except to change your focus and begin to look forward.

No husband is perfect. Even Jesus didn't have perfect parents on earth. No brothers and sisters get along all the time. Friendships have ups and downs and ins and outs. Nothing in your life will be exactly as you dreamed, wished, or planned.

I just telephoned a friend whom I haven't seen in a long time because we once had a major conflict. I invited her to lunch. I decided I want to be the first to reconcile. I'll spend some time praying for her first, and I'll bring the chocolate—Godiva, of course.

Bringing the Chocolate

1. Read the book of Jonah (it's only four chapters long). Why did Jonah pout on the hillside? Can you see yourself sitting beside him? Ask God what to do about the pain you feel.

2. Are you ready to pray God's blessings on someone who hurt you? If so, start now. If not, ask God to fill you with grace and mercy toward that person.

3. Does God's continued forgiveness of Israel's failures and Jesus's "seventy-seven times" attitude about forgiveness cause you to reconsider your feelings toward someone who hurt you? How does the scripture make you feel about how much God loves you?

4. What in this chapter helped you to think about forgiveness in a new way?

Prayer

*Dear Lord, may Your forgiveness fill me to overflowing
so that I will be a forgiving friend.*

Offering Chocolate to My Friend

Dear friend, yes, I forgive you before you even ask.

Good-as-Godiva Chocolate Cheesecake

Crust:

1 1/2 cups finely crushed Oreos

1 1/2 tablespoons granulated sugar

4 tablespoons unsalted butter, melted

Directions:

Mix together sugar and Oreos. Pour melted butter over the

mixture and stir until completely moistened. Press evenly into the bottom of a springform pan. Set aside.

Filling:

4 8-oz. packages cream cheese, softened

2 1-oz. squares unsweetened chocolate, finely chopped

1/3 cup all-purpose flour

1 14-oz. can sweetened condensed milk

2 large eggs

Directions:

Preheat oven to 350°F.

Beat cream cheese until smooth. Add flour and sweetened condensed milk; beat until smooth. Add eggs, one at a time, and beat well.

In a clean, dry, microwave-safe bowl, melt the unsweetened chocolate for ten seconds. Stir well and, if still not melted, microwave again in five-second intervals. Add melted chocolate and blend. Pour over crumb crust in prepared springform pan and bake for forty-five minutes or until center is set. Transfer to a wire rack to cool, then chill in refrigerator.

Chocolate-Cream Pie with Loyalty Meringue

A gossip betrays a confidence,
but a trustworthy man keeps a secret.
PROVERBS 11:13

What you see before you, my friend,
is the result of a lifetime of chocolate.
KATHARINE HEPBURN

In a cooking class I took in high school, our teacher taught us proper culinary techniques like precise measuring and how to follow instructions such as sauté, fold, blanch, julienne, dredge, and mince. Most of the terms and methods I've since forgotten, but one of the recipes became a family classic: chocolate-cream pie with fluffy meringue topping. Whenever I bake this luscious, rich, creamy dessert, my family devours it.

The recipe itself contains meticulous instructions like tempering the egg yolks before incorporating them into the hot filling and bringing egg whites to room temperature before whipping. I've discovered that if I want the pie to turn out perfect, each detail must be followed carefully. The meringue layer is especially sensitive—proportions must be balanced, and ingredients added at precise intervals. The delicate mixture requires gentle handling. Cutting corners will result in a fiasco.

In much the same way, loyalty—a crucial ingredient in any friendship—requires consistent care or it will deflate like a poorly handled meringue. *True* friends choose loyalty over condemnation. It may be tempting to assume the worst when you hear a rumor about a friend. But if you counter the innuendo with a balance of fidelity and support and temper it with love, you cover that relationship with loyalty that stands tall and beautiful, like fluffy meringue on a chocolate pie.

LOYALTY ENCOURAGES

Each of us has been wrong at some point, whether in action or speech. When we are wrong, we need a loyal encourager.

The apostle Paul, after receiving word about the moral wrongs infiltrating the Corinthian church, wrote the letter we know as First Corinthians. Paul wanted to help the people of that church recognize the immorality seeping through their congregation. In his letter, Paul urges the Corinthians to repent and seek change. Read casually or out of context, the letter sounds harsh and judgmental; but if you study the words and the tone, you discover an undercurrent of fierce loyalty that proves Paul's great love for the people of Corinth.

When Paul wrote his second letter to the Corinthians, many of the problems had been resolved. Paul apologized for his harsh words and assured the Corinthians of his great loyalty to them: "I do not say this to condemn you; I have said before that you have such a place in our hearts that we would live or die with you. I have great confidence in you; I take great pride in you. I am greatly encouraged; in all our troubles my joy knows no bounds."[1]

As a pastor, leader, and apostle, Paul was obligated to point out the mistakes of the Corinthians. But his correction overflowed with love as rich as chocolate topped with loyalty like golden meringue. Notice Paul's words of love, allegiance, and affirmation. Pride. Confidence. Joy. Even through their failure and uncertainty, Paul was loyal to them.

Loyal encouragement is just as necessary when we ourselves have been wronged. Remember the friendship of David and Jonathan from 1 Samuel 19? Saul, Jonathan's father and the king of Israel, had arbitrarily convicted David of treason and condemned him to death. Jonathan put himself in grave danger by going to his father and proclaiming David's innocence. In other words, Jonathan chose loyalty over the easy way out. The politically correct thing to do would have been to agree with his father. Instead, he chose to be loyal to his friend.

Like Jonathan, you and I must become defense lawyers for

our friends. When the talk turns negative, speak up for your friend by stating the positive.

LOYALTY LISTENS

In an article about friendship, writer Margo Jefferson describes her friend Ingrid in *O, The Oprah Magazine:* "I was obsessed with being a perfect writer. And I was terrified that I could never live up to my own ambitions.... I confided all this to Ingrid during those years. I don't remember what she said. I remember that she listened."[2]

> A hug is worth a thousand words. A friend is worth more.
> —AUTHOR UNKNOWN

Every girl needs a girlfriend she can confide in, someone who will really listen. How are your listening skills? When a friend shares her fears or struggles, are you subconsciously making your grocery list? Are you thinking about what you're going to say next?

C. S. Lewis's father, Albert, had difficulty truly listening to others. Lewis wrote that he could tell his father "that a boy called Churchwood had caught a field mouse and kept it as a pet, and a year, or ten years later, he would ask you, 'Did you ever hear what became of poor Chickweed who was so afraid of the rats?'"[3] Inability to listen is a barrier to communication.

We need someone to listen to us carefully. We need girlfriends who don't simply focus on themselves while we share our inner thoughts and struggles.

There's a funny scene in an episode of *Everybody Loves Raymond* where Raymond accompanies his father and his father's old cronies to the steam room at the lodge. When anyone mentions an illness or pain, one of the old guys responds in a monotone that he knows every misery:

"I have a pain in my knee."

"Yeah, I got that."

"My shoulder hurts."

"Yeah, I got that."

This guy never recognizes that the other person is in pain. He focuses only on himself.

It is a rare friend who puts every thought from her own mind and focuses on her friend. A listening friend hears the words and perceives the heart. We get a glimpse of how important this is in Margo Jefferson's *O* article: "Ingrid had decided to treat my life with a respect that I was not capable of."[4]

Respect is the key to becoming a listener. If you respect and admire your friend, you honor her through courtesy and consideration. This means regarding her so highly that you defer your own information, thoughts, and advice and allow her to express herself fully. Do you respect your friend enough to listen to her words? And not just listen, but also *hear* the emotion and conflict beneath her words? True loyalty means learning to listen.

LOYAL ENOUGH TO TELL THE TRUTH

Karen Lassiter Kerber, my friend and former college roommate, came to visit George and me not long after the birth of our first child.

At the time, Karen was still attending university and dressed in the latest styles. I, on the other hand, had been wearing nothing but maternity clothes for months and was just beginning to fit back into my old clothes. This was when miniskirts and platform shoes were in vogue; compared to Karen, I looked downright frumpy in my long prepregnancy skirts. Karen wasn't about to let me continue looking out of date, so before she left that weekend, we hemmed all my skirts and dresses to a stylish above-the-knee length.

Like Eva Gabor sang in the theme song from *Green Acres,* "Darlin', I love ya, but give me Park Avenue," Karen said to me, "Darlin', I love ya, but you've got to do something about that dress." Or as Valerie Monroe wrote in *O, The Oprah Magazine,* "Friends don't let friends go out in those Dame Edna glasses…that alien hair color…those stripes."[5]

WHEN LOYALTY DOESN'T COME NATURALLY

One of the most difficult things for me to do is show loyalty to a friend who is depressed.

My personality type is a combination of choleric (strong,

decisive, worker bee) and sanguine (looking for fun in every situation). My natural response to depression is to say, "Snap out of it!" I tend to suggest (sometimes not too sweetly) that my friends stop looking at the negative side of things and adopt a more positive, hope-filled position.

But if I am loyal to my friend, I try to understand her feelings. Unfortunately, depression—whether clinical and long-term or circumstantial and short-term—tends to isolate women, leaving them more alone than ever. If we choose to cover friendships with loyalty meringue, we won't allow our friend to go through depression alone. True loyalty walks in when everyone else walks out.

God knew I needed to develop more compassion toward my friends who walk through the shadows of depression, so last year He allowed me to experience firsthand how depression feels. I am thankful I was mired only temporarily in that slough. This excerpt from my journal offers a snapshot of the depths to which I plunged.

What is wrong with me? I am lethargic. No energy. No ambition and no fire in my everyday life. I want to sleep all the time. Is it physical? What?

I feel like a failure and yet I don't seem to care. There are no new prospects or positive responses from any proposal I make. Can I really do anything? Why am I so driven? Why am I not satisfied? Everything's a mess and I feel alone.

> *I hurt all over, especially my legs. The*
> *scariest thing is that I have no self-confidence.*
> *So unlikely that I should feel this way. I've*
> *never had a single time that I can ever remember*
> *when I thought I was incapable. Until now.*

I felt alone, paralyzed.

During this time I traveled to Canada for a week to stay with my precious grandchildren while my son and daughter-in-law attended a missionary orientation. Toronto is a huge city, and I felt as if I'd been thrown into a massive, unfamiliar cavern. I was terrified even to drive to the grocery store; I worried I would get lost trying to find my way back or that I would get into a car accident. I fretted over whether I could properly care for my grandchildren.

Those who know me well would be shocked to learn the depths of my insecurities and depression because I work very hard to appear confident and positive. Yet beneath this facade lay the fear that most of my friends would laugh if they could see my pity party.

Before I left for Canada, I e-mailed a friend I know casually, Leslie Vernick, a licensed counselor who wrote the book *Getting Over the Blues.* When I told Leslie about my horrible feelings, she didn't condemn me, or laugh (as I secretly feared my friends would do), or tell me to "straighten up." Instead she encouraged me and sent me a copy of her book. As I read it on the plane ride to Canada, I recognized in myself the signs of depression. Even as I wondered why this happened to me, I reveled in the support that Leslie had shown.

Today when I see Leslie at events sponsored by a professional author/speaker group that we belong to, she hugs me and encourages me. Though we have many mutual friends, she has never told another person about my difficulties. Her loyalty to me is like meringue on a chocolate-cream pie—beautiful and tasty.

> If you are not feeling well, if you have not slept, chocolate will revive you. But you have no chocolate! I think of that again and again! My dear, how will you ever manage?
> —MARQUISE DE SEVIGNE

One afternoon in Canada, while my youngest grandbaby napped and the oldest was still at school, I called another friend, Lori. She and her family were still hunkered down in the safety of a northern Louisiana country home, having fled Hurricane Rita as it ripped across east Texas. We talked for a while about where various family and friends had sought refuge from the storm. After a while, Lori sensed my struggle and coaxed it out of me. When I finally broke down and told her about my fears, she prayed for me right then and there. She prayed that God would show me His hand and His plans.

Though Lori faced agonizing uncertainties of her own, including not even knowing whether her house would be standing when she returned home, she listened to me and heaped on incredible mounds of loyalty meringue.

PAUL IN THE DEPTHS

The apostle Paul faced persecution in many of the cities where he preached. I've often thought about how anxious and overwhelmed he must have felt. It's probable that he was sinking into depression when he wrote, "For when we came into Macedonia, this body of ours had no rest, but we were harassed at every turn—conflicts on the outside, fears within."[6]

Can you imagine how Paul must have felt? His words sound like my journal entry. Like me, he was tired, stressed, and insecure. But his friends were loyal, and the concern and love they showed caused him to turn to joy instead of depression. "But God, who comforts the downcast, comforted us by the coming of Titus, and not only by his coming but also by the comfort you had given him. He told us about your longing for me, your deep sorrow, your ardent concern for me, so that my joy was greater than ever."[7]

When life overwhelms and confuses us, loyal friends bring us joy and peace.

WHAT LOYALTY COULD DO

Something wicked inside human beings makes us love bad news and gossip. What do you think would happen if Christians believed only the best about others?

Eddie is a pastor who finds dealing with insincere, power-hungry people the worst part of his job. Recently he began to feel the burnout that often accompanies stress and constant activity. He loved the people in the church and the strong calling of God to pastor, but part of him wanted to quit and walk away.

Then one Sunday morning when Eddie arrived at church, a deacon who rarely attended was waiting for him. "Pastor, I heard that the audit isn't finished yet. What's going on? Is someone trying to hide something?"

Eddie tried to explain, but the man stormed away in a huff.

The morning service was about to begin when another man approached him. "Pastor, I visited a church across town last week, and it was so exciting. They had a band and great music. And that pastor can really preach. We need something fresh like that around here."

Eddie could hardly lift his feet as he made his way up to the pulpit to begin the morning service. He looked over the crowd. Not a smile on a face. The music began, but Eddie heard a requiem. He couldn't remember what he spoke in the sermon. At the close of the service, a lady spoke up. "Some of us are going to form a new church in the south city area. If any of you want to join us, meet at my house tonight."

Just a few disloyal church members convinced Eddie to resign the pastorate.

What if those members had chosen loyalty instead? What if

the angry man had said, "Pastor, can I do anything to help in the office?" What if the member who loved lively worship had volunteered to organize a band or paid the pastor's expenses to a conference on worship? What if he had come to the office the following week to pray with and encourage Eddie? What if the enthusiastic lady had worked in conjunction with Eddie and his staff to develop church ministry in a new city area?

Loyalty considers others before acting.

LOYAL IN ALL CIRCUMSTANCES

One morning Vickie's husband told her he wanted a divorce. He was tired of the hassle of marriage and family and wanted his freedom. He was worn out from the stress of his job, finances, and responsibilities. Someone new had made him feel young, handsome, and less stressed.

After he left, Vickie sat in shock. *God, please tell someone to call me. I need a friend.*

Barbara was sitting at her office desk when she suddenly felt an urge to call Vickie.

"Hello?"

"Vickie, it's Barbara. Is everything okay?"

Vickie began to sob. "No," she said. "My life just fell apart. Mike asked me for a divorce."

Barbara immediately drove to Vickie's house and found her in an emotional heap on the sofa. Before long, more friends came. The conversations and prayers over the next several days and nights were centered on how Vickie could cope through her devastation, fear, and hurt.

It would have been easy for Vickie's friends to throw degrading insults at her husband. But instead they focused on loving and caring for Vickie.

But these friends' loyalty didn't stop with Vickie. Not only did they rally around Vickie, but they also showered Mike with love and concern. They never told him he was a failure or called him names. Instead, friends spoke truth to him and told him that his feelings were not so unusual. They also helped him see that feelings can be deceptive and what really matters is what God thinks of our feelings. These loving, loyal friends opened the door to God's thoughts for Mike. They urged him to view his marriage from God's perspective.

Even Vickie's family ministered to Mike. The family didn't call him names or plot revenge. Vickie's mother could have vowed never to speak to Mike again for hurting her daughter, but instead she called Mike and expressed her love, concern, encouragement, understanding, and forgiveness.

A few months later, when Vickie and Mike reconciled and the marriage-healing process began, their friends regretted nothing. And Mike says he is so grateful to Vickie's family for acceptance with no strings attached. When the marriage healed, friendships and family relationships with the couple were unharmed and unencumbered because of loyalty.

When circumstances are at their worst, loyal friends don't give up. No obstacle is too great for a friend who is genuinely loyal.

LOYALTY PRAYS AND DOESN'T GOSSIP

One of the greatest things we can do in Christian circles is pray together. But if we aren't loyal in our prayer-request time, this marvelous tool and pathway to God and His blessings can become nothing more than a poor excuse for gossip.

Sometimes it is so heady and invigorating to know a secret that we can hardly resist telling. Sharing secrets about another girlfriend's pain, even as a prayer request, is selfish. We know we shouldn't talk about it but we want everyone to see that we are "in the know."

A friendship covered in loyalty meringue never speaks of a friend's troubles. Since prayer is so important, we *should* ask others to pray. But instead of speaking the name, speak the problem: "I know someone who's struggling with alcohol. Please pray that she will get professional help and that I can be a loyal friend to her through this difficult time." "My friend's husband left her. Please pray that God will be close to her and that I can be a true friend."

In some cases it's okay to ask permission to share your friend's difficulties with a prayer group. But loyalty prohibits sharing without consent.

Our friendship compels us to be loyal in spite of rumors. In every situation, we should ask how we can rescue our friend from the scandal machine. Just as the tiniest bit of yolk in the egg whites will ruin your meringue, even a few words of gossip can destroy a friendship. There is power of life and death in the tongue.

LOYALTY DEFENDS

I read a story about a mother who took her daughter to the doctor for a physical. Some tests indicated pregnancy. The daughter pleaded with her mother to believe the test was wrong and that pregnancy was impossible. The mother asked the doctor to run the test again because there must be some mistake. I don't remember the results, and it doesn't matter. The important thing is that in that moment, the young girl knew her mother's loyalty.

> Chocolate in the morning is what makes moms get through their day!
>
> —AUTHOR UNKNOWN

I once spoke at a retreat and shared this story as an example of loyalty. Afterward, a woman came to me with tears in her eyes. She told me she was facing a similar situation. My illustration had reminded her that loyalty to her daughter was more important than what anyone else thought. She would choose loyalty over suspicion. We talked about the possibility of her daughter's test returning positive and prayed together that this mother wouldn't find herself in denial but would stick up for her child with great love and loyalty, even if the results were distressing.

A LOYAL FRIEND

Near the fence behind my parents' house grows a beautiful stand of lilies, and every spring they bloom red, yellow, purple, and orange. I don't know how they survived. Years ago Mom dug them up at Grandmother's house to bring them here, but she forgot to plant them for much too long. We finally got them in the flower bed, and miraculously they lived; but later the cows leaned over the fence and chewed them to the ground. Just when they sprang up again, Dad mowed them flat. We've forgotten to water or feed them plenty of times, and now weeds surround them. Yet there they are—blooming brilliantly, as beautiful as if Someone "reached down"[8] and pulled them up to stand straight and glorious.

> If it ain't chocolate,
> it ain't breakfast!
> —AUTHOR UNKNOWN

When I feel as though I've been chewed down to the nub…when careless words mow me down…when I allow anger, impatience, or unforgiveness to rule my day…when weeds creep in, I need a friend. A girlfriend who sees my potential, not my failures, who willingly reaches down to pull me up.

Loyal friendship, as luscious as chocolate pie with meringue, is only possible if I am willing to reach into the messiness of my friend's life and help her survive and blossom.

What might another person be if you were really loyal to her?

I wonder how my former secretary, Shirley, who got strung out on drugs, would have reacted if I'd kept going to her apartment and calling her. What if I had encouraged her to get into a treatment program? What if I had been merciful enough to show her I cared and strong enough not to enable her? What if I hadn't walked out of her life like I did?

I wonder if Annie's life would be different today if I had not given up on her when she left her husband and kids for her old high-school flame. We served on committees and ministry teams together, but after her affair I washed my hands of our friendship. What if I had been loyal? What if I chose to look past her pain through the lens of my own mistakes, knowing that my failures (mask and minimize them though I try) are no less than hers?

Would Shirley or Annie have given up on God if I hadn't given up on them? Would they be like Grandmother's lilies—beaten down but not destroyed?

I never again want to be one who deserts friends. When my friend needs me the most, I have an opportunity to be the light shining in her darkness. With God's help I can follow the advice in Proverbs. "Never abandon a friend."[9] Loyalty is the consistent and constant support that says, "I'll defend you." Loyalty is showing sincere and unshakable belief in my friend.

Bringing the Chocolate

1. Read 2 Corinthians 7. How did Paul show his loyalty to the Corinthians? List at least three things you can do to be more loyal to your friends.

2. Why is listening so important in loyal friendship? What can you do to develop better listening skills?

3. Do you know a friend who is prone to days or weeks of depression? What can you do to be loyal to her?

4. Do you know someone who has been beaten down and chewed up by circumstances or people? What actions might you take to prove your loyalty?

Prayer
Dear Lord, when I am ready to judge and condemn,
remind me to choose loyalty instead.

Offering Chocolate to My Friend
Dear friend, I'll be loyal to you
even if all the evidence condemns you.

Chocolate-Cream Pie
Makes one 9-inch pie.
Crust:
1 cup all-purpose flour
1/3 cup shortening, chilled

1/2 teaspoon salt

2 tablespoons ice water

Directions:

Sift flour into a mixing bowl. Cut in shortening with a pastry blender or two table knives until the mixture resembles the consistency of small peas. Sprinkle the water a tablespoon at a time over the flour-shortening mixture; mix gently.

Gather the dough into a ball. Roll from center to edge into a circle one inch larger than your pie plate; use quick, light strokes and release pressure at the edge. Transfer the dough loosely to a nine-inch pie plate, trimming overhanging about one-and-one-half inches past the edge. Fold extra pastry under and flute decoratively. Use a fork to prick small holes in the bottom and sides of the piecrust. Bake at 425°F for five to eight minutes, until lightly browned. Remove from oven and cool. Lower oven temperature to 350°F.

Note: There are many wonderful ready-to-bake frozen and refrigerated piecrusts available in the supermarket. I often use these products successfully.

Cream Pie:

1/3 cup all-purpose flour or 1/4 cup cornstarch

1 cup granulated sugar

1/4 teaspoon salt

3 tablespoons unsweetened cocoa powder

3 tablespoons unsalted butter, divided

2 cups whole milk

3 egg yolks (reserve whites for meringue)

1 teaspoon pure vanilla extract

Directions:

Combine flour, sugar, salt, cocoa, and one tablespoon of butter in a saucepan.

In a separate saucepan, scald the milk by placing it over medium heat; when the milk is hot but not boiling, test with a spoon. If it coats the spoon, it is ready.

Whisk the scalded milk into the dry ingredients and bring the mixture to a boil. Cook for two minutes (mixture will thicken to a puddinglike consistency). Remove from heat.

Whisk the egg yolks in a separate bowl, then slowly add about one-half cup of the hot milk mixture, whisking constantly. When the mixture is smooth, pour the egg yolk mixture back into the remaining hot milk mixture. (*This may seem like a strange step, but if you pour cold egg yolks directly into the hot mixture, you will end up with scrambled eggs. This step—"tempering"—brings the yolks closer to the desired temperature before you combine the two.*) Return the pan to medium heat and cook one minute, stirring constantly. Remove from heat.

Whisk in the remaining two tablespoons of butter and the vanilla. Cool slightly, then pour the mixture into the baked pastry shell.

Meringue:

3 egg whites, room temperature

1/4 teaspoon salt
1/4 teaspoon cream of tartar
6 tablespoons granulated sugar
1 teaspoon pure vanilla extract
Directions:

Make sure that your egg whites are completely free of yolks. Combine the whites with the salt and cream of tartar in the bowl of an electric mixer; beat until frothy. Add sugar, one tablespoon at a time. Beat until stiff and glossy. (Meringue is ready for pie when sugar has dissolved and meringue is stiff enough to hold a peak, yet still looks moist.)

Gently fold in vanilla. Cover the top of the pie with the meringue, using a spoon to seal the edges and make fluffy peaks over the surface.

Bake in 350°F oven for ten to twelve minutes, until meringue is lightly browned.

Chocolate-Fountain Joy

Perfume and incense bring joy to the heart,
and the pleasantness of one's friend
springs from his earnest counsel.

PROVERBS 27:9

I never met a chocolate I didn't like.
DEANNA TROI, *STAR TREK: THE NEXT GENERATION*

My daughter, Cherry, owns a catering company called Elegant Events. One of her most popular pieces of equipment is a large chocolate fountain. When she sets that fountain up at an event, the sight, sound, and aroma really get people's attention. Like a pied piper, the promise of chocolate calls to guests. Cherry surrounds the fountain with trays full of strawberries, bananas, cantaloupe, pineapple, and grapes, along with mountains of marshmallows, cookies, wafers, and pretzels. As the creamy chocolate flows over the curves of the fountain, guests share in the joy of trying something new in the bubbling flow. Strawberries and bananas are always a hit, but everyone is surprised by the extraordinary taste of a grape coated with chocolate. Marshmallows and Oreo cookies are also favorites. Sometimes Cherry will pile a stack of small chocolate candies on the trays; everyone agrees that even chocolate tastes better when dipped in chocolate.

As Christ followers, we have every reason to be joyful. The world is more beautiful because we know the Creator. The sights, sounds, and smells of life command our delighted attention. We automatically develop a curiosity and interest in people. Joy bubbles over in us like a chocolate fountain. Our happiness spills in great rivulets, covering everyone around us.

GOD KNOWS JOY

God knows joy. The Bible says that He rejoices in His works of creation. Imagine His delight in the beginning, when He flung the stars and set the sun in place. And according to Isaiah, God can hardly wait to show us His new heavens and earth. "I will rejoice over Jerusalem and take delight in my people."[1] God experiences joy and satisfaction over His creation, His people, and His plans for His people.

The Bible is filled with joyful events. Joy came to the earth when Jesus Christ left His throne in heaven and became a human. The angels announced Jesus's birth to the shepherds by saying, "I bring you good news of great joy."[2] When the wise men "saw the star, they were overjoyed."[3] The night Jesus was born, the angels held a party in the sky. Can you envision the pyrotechnic light show over Bethlehem? Jesus said that heaven rejoices when even one sinner repents.

There's an important difference between joy and pleasure. Pleasure centers on what makes me feel good, but it doesn't guarantee joy. A life that is "all about me" and indulges all my wants and desires is a dead, dull life because it is so limited.

Real joy is the result of knowing and serving God. It can be found nowhere else. There is only one source for joy: God. So know Him. Serve Him. And joy will fill you up.

When your relationship with God is right, joy is the result. Whether you are blessed or persecuted, joy follows. Even in troubled situations, persecution, or death, we experience pain and hurt, but because we know God, joy comes bubbling up like a chocolate fountain. "Count yourselves blessed every time people put you down or throw you out or speak lies about you to

> Chocolate doesn't make the world go 'round, but it certainly makes the ride worthwhile.
> —AUTHOR UNKNOWN

discredit me. What it means is that the truth is too close for comfort and they are uncomfortable. You can be glad when that happens—give a cheer, even!—for though they don't like it, *I* do! And all heaven applauds. And know that you are in good company. My prophets and witnesses have always gotten into this kind of trouble."[4]

At Pisidian Antioch, the disciples were run out of town, but they were filled with joy because joy doesn't depend on acceptance, rejection, or any other circumstance.[5]

In the worst of situations, joy shines through. Author Joyce Landorf wrote a compelling book about her mother's death, *Mourning Song*. Toward the beginning of her illness, Joyce's mother told her, "Joyce honey, pull up a chair and get a pad of paper. I've shown you how to live, now I'm going to show you how to die."[6] In the next months, her mother helped Joyce understand the intricacies of finding joy in whatever situation life brings. She left Joyce with a legacy of exuberant joy even in her illness.

WHERE TO FIND JOY

To learn what people are saying about deep, heartfelt happiness on the Internet, I did a Google search on the word *joy*. My search came back with *more than 200 million* results. I discovered Web sites devoted to the joy of painting, joy of cooking, joy of aerobics, joy of scrapbooking, joy of hand spinning, and even joy of cloth diapers. *(What are they thinking?)* There's a jumping for joy competitive jump-rope team, books with the word *joy* in the title, people named Joy, a rock band called Joy, and even a song titled "Joy" by Michael Jackson. I found at least two churches named Joy Church and even a Web site called Joy of Pigs, dedicated to the poor misunderstood mammals. But my favorite was a site devoted totally to Almond Joy chocolate candy bars. *Sometimes you feel like a nut.*

I shouldn't have been surprised to discover that on the Internet, joy is often related to an activity or a possession. Certainly our culture pushes us to grab all the gusto in life and buy as many toys and pretty things as we can. But as Christ followers, we know that joy has nothing to do with stuff, money, or meaningless activities. Our joy starts deep and swells up inside us until we can't hold it in any longer. That's when zest for life shows up in our face and in all we do.

> Chocolate:
> Here today...
> gone today!
> —AUTHOR UNKNOWN

Before joy can spread to our relationships with our friends, it has to come from our relationship with God. When my personal relationship with God is strong, it is sweet—like a strawberry dipped in a flowing chocolate fountain. Friendships thrive and satisfy when we cover the relationship with the joy of knowing God.

When I searched the New Testament for instances of the word *joy,* I realized God sent joy to earth in the bodily form of Jesus, so we could experience it and relish the thrill of knowing Him.[7] Jesus's followers also experienced great joy when other people heard and received the gospel. In Acts 8:8, Phillip preached in Samaria; when the people accepted Christ, "there was great joy in that city."

True joy comes only through Jesus; He is the joy of our salvation. When we have Him, we have joy. We can then spread that joy by spreading news of His love.

Joy Is for Sharing

When I first started traveling for my company, I was sent to Paris, France. After my meetings were over, I walked the magnificent streets in the beautiful city on the River Seine. I was awestruck when I rounded a corner and saw the open spaces of the Place de la Concorde with Cleopatra's Needle.

But I was alone. No one was there to share the incredible sight.

I continued walking toward the Arc de Triomphe and the Tour Eiffel—I could see the top of each structure from the Champs Élysées. But no one shared those highlights with me. The city's beauty and grandeur fizzled because I had no one to revel in it with.

A few weeks ago, Cherry and I went to the Nutcracker Market in Houston. The beautiful wares of the crafty and creative were almost more than our eyes could take in. But the gladness of our hearts wasn't because of the merchandise; it was because we were there together.

Joy is meant to be relished with others, shared bliss with a friend. Though we know joy because of the abundant life we've been given in Jesus, it really isn't full-blown until we share it with someone.

THE CHOCOLATE FOUNTAIN OF JOY

A chocolate fountain is an incredible thing. Here's how it works: as the machine pumps the melted chocolate up through a center column, the chocolate flows past the top tier, over the medium tier, and finally down the largest tier, coming to rest in a pool at the bottom. Since the chocolate flows in a continuous stream like a rich waterfall, the three tiers seem almost connected.

A joy-filled friendship, I've discovered, is also built on three tiers.

1. Laughter

Nothing is better for a friendship than a good belly laugh. Some friends make you laugh...and laugh...and laugh. If you call them up, you already know you are going to laugh.

My daddy's four sisters were best friends with each other. With them, life was always about laughter. Everything was funny. They saw something hilarious in every situation and couldn't wait to tell the others. My aunts retold the stories so often that I knew the details as if I had been there. No matter how many times one sister repeated a story, the laughter never lessened. In fact, the more often a story was retold, the funnier it got. Sometimes one of the sisters would only have to say one word, and the whole room would double over in laughter.

The Bible gives us advice on laughter. "Laugh with your happy friends when they're happy; share tears when they're down."[8] All situations require joy. Notice the advice to "share" happy laughter as well as tears. Both are a part of the joy of friendship.

W. H. Auden once wrote, "Among those whom I like or admire, I can find no common denominator; but among those whom I love, I can: All of them make me laugh."

Friendship needs laughter. It is the key to rich, enduring, joyful relationships. Everyone could use more laughter and joy in their lives. Pastor John Ortberg says, "One hunger is universal. You have never met a person who doesn't long for more joy. More often than you can imagine when people are stressed, worried, preoccupied, lonely, or afraid, they carry this sign just beneath the surface: 'Joy needed—please lighten up.'"[9]

> Chocolate is a perfect food, as wholesome as it is delicious.
> —AUTHOR UNKNOWN

When I know I'm going to get together with girlfriends on a road trip or a retreat, I get absolutely giddy with anticipation. I know we are going to spend time laughing and thoroughly delighting in one another. Just the thought entices me like a flowing chocolate fountain.

When our group of writer friends gets together once a

month, I know we are going to spend some of our time laughing together. It's a part of being friends and knowing each other's likes, dislikes, habits, and traits. When we read what each has written, we enjoy the thoughts and words. Every nuance of humor is easily detected because of the friendship we share.

I serve on the staff of C.L.A.S.S., a program for speakers and writers. At a recent conference I roomed with Kathryn Robbins, whom I'd met but didn't know well. In the middle of the night, my iPod (for no good reason we could figure out) came on in my purse. The machine was tuned to a Christian radio talk show that I'd downloaded, so what we heard in our dark, silent room was a conversation. We both awoke and tried to figure out if the voices were coming from the hallway or outside the window. Finally, we realized the sound came from my purse. After I opened my bag and turned off the offending iPod, we laughed for the rest of the night—spontaneously, uncontrollably, hysterically, involuntarily. Yes, we were tired the next day. But our new friendship is forever engraved with that night of laughter.

Nothing gets a friendship going like shared laughter. The quality of a friendship can be measured by the volume and depth of your laughter.

2. Perspective

This second tier is about how we see things. Viewpoint. In rich friendship, everything is viewed with cheer. The Bible says, "Everything God created is good, and to be received with thanks.

Nothing is to be sneered at and thrown out."[10] The good and the bad are to be received with joy.

I received an e-mail from my friend Donna Gilmer. It read, "I think of you often and frankly, when I do…I laugh out loud."

Donna didn't know it, but her e-mail altered my life. Until I received that e-mail, I groused around my everyday life, grumbling, complaining, and feeling sorry for myself. *I have too much to do at work and at home. No one appreciates what I do. The office work goes unrecognized, and the housework has to be repeated the next day.* Not only did I feel unloved and unappreciated, I was spreading the misery around to coworkers and family. Barking orders and complaining.

> Exercise is a dirty word…
> every time I hear it, I wash
> my mouth out with chocolate.
> —AUTHOR UNKNOWN

But Donna and I hadn't seen each other in a while. She doesn't know this depressing, whining side of me. When she thinks of me, she bursts out laughing because of the fun times we've shared. Because of the work we've accomplished in women's ministry and in Bible-study groups. Because knowing Jesus and seeing Him work is delightful. Because of the craziness of our sanguine wardrobes and earrings. Because of the perspective of joy.

Donna's e-mail made me step back and take a good look at how I'd been behaving. Why was I whining and acting like a slug? From the correct perspective, I see that my life is wonderful. I've enjoyed a fabulous career, and those dishes and floors at home are a blessing from God.

It's all about perspective, girls. Sometimes it takes a friend like Donna to help me see life like a chocolate fountain and get a joyful viewpoint.

3. Spiritual Sharing

When two girlfriends are on a common spiritual path toward stronger faith, joy flows over the friendship.

Sometimes my friend Edith will call me because she spent her morning in prayer and Bible study. Some stress she faced that day is made clearer or easier because of how the Word comforted her, and she can't wait to share what she learned with me.

How we relate spiritually to our friends is either going to increase or diminish our joy. If we determine to become spiritual sisters, we will build our friends up by sharing what we've learned on our own spiritual journey. The heart is happiest when it beats for others.

My friend Edna Ellison has written several books in the Friend to Friend series. The idea behind the books is for two friends to spend time together with a special emphasis on sharing the Scriptures: "Grab a cup of coffee and your Bible and meet your girlfriend at the park." Edna's books recognize the need for friends to connect spiritually and deeply. True joy spills into the relationship when we do.

Laughter and perspective are delightful elements of friendship. But when we share a common love of God, drench ourselves in truth from the Word, and cover it with the Holy Spirit...friendship becomes joy.

CHOOSE JOY

Don't let anything cause you to lose joy. When circumstances are painful or stressful, it is easy to let the wear and tear of simply surviving steal your joy. Joyful living becomes a conscious decision; it means *choosing* joy...even when we may not feel like it.

When the pioneers crossed the plains in covered wagons, they would sometimes see fires in the distance sweeping across the prairie. Such fires, driven by the wind, threatened everything in the path of the flames. In defense, the pioneers would set another fire nearby to burn off a patch of ground. Then they would pull the wagons into the burned-out area. The big fire could find nothing left to ignite there, so they were safe.

In the same way, we need to build a safe place that doesn't allow anything, anyone, or any situation to steal our joy. We build this safe place by practicing the art of *choosing joy*.

When stress at work overwhelms you, choose joy. When illness shatters your peaceful plans, choose joy. When your finances are skimpy, choose joy. When families clash, choose joy. When disappointments hover, choose joy. When you make the premeditated, calculated decision to be joyful, you pull your friends into your safe place. That's chocolate-fountain joy.

Some of my friends and I laugh about the lower jaw jowls that we all seem to acquire as we get older. Short of plastic surgery, what can we do? We have discovered that a big smile will hoist up the drooping flesh like an instant face-lift.

Smile. Turns out this maneuver is also a practical way to choose joy. If you are joyful, smile. And if you don't feel so joyful, smile anyway. A smile will bring out the joy. (Besides, you look better.)

When George and I visited New York City, we got tickets to see the revival of the musical *Oklahoma!* We loved the sets, costumes, and the brilliant music of Rodgers and Hammerstein. No matter what trouble the characters got themselves into, there was a song and dance that fit the occasion. It's a good example for us to follow. When in trouble, strike up the band! Bring on the music! The Bible says, "My dear, dear friends! I love you so much. I do want the very best for you. You make me feel such joy, fill me with such pride. Don't waver. Stay on track, steady in God."[11]

Fostering sweet fellowship with friends is the key to experiencing chocolate-fountain joy. Friendships are richer, deeper, and more fun when friends choose joy.

Bringing the Chocolate

1. Read Matthew 5:11–12 in as many different translations or versions as you can find (go to crosswalk.com for access to numerous selections). Embrace the words of Jesus for any hurtful situation in your life that is trying to steal your joy.

2. How would you describe your relationship with God? What can you do to strengthen it?

3. Think of a time when you and a girlfriend laughed together uncontrollably. Call her up and remind her. Laugh again.

4. What or who is trying to steal your joy? What steps will you take to protect yourself from joy stealers?

Prayer

*Dear Lord, help me keep my relationship with You open
and active so that my relationships with my friends
will be filled with joy.*

Offering Chocolate to My Friend

Dear friend, I promise to laugh
and choose joy in our friendship.

Chocolate-Fountain Fondue

*If you want to enjoy the fun in your home, purchase a small
chocolate fountain—they are sold in specialty stores and online.*

But even if you don't have a chocolate fountain, you can enjoy the fun of a chocolate fondue with your friends.

Ingredients:

1 cup heavy cream

12 ounces semisweet chocolate chips

1 teaspoon pure vanilla extract

Directions:

In a saucepan, combine the heavy cream with the chocolate chips. Slowly melt the chips over medium heat, stirring often; when mixture is smooth, add vanilla.

This chocolate sauce may be served in a fondue pot or doubled and served in a small chocolate fountain. If the mixture is too thick for dipping, thin to the correct consistency by adding small amounts of cream.

Freedom Is Like a Box of Chocolates

Don't wreck a sublime chocolate
experience by feeling guilty.
LORA BRODY

As iron sharpens iron, so one man sharpens another.
PROVERBS 27:17

The beautiful shapes in a box of chocolates amaze me. Little shells, flowers, boxes, pyramids, and balls—what a beautiful sight to open and ogle. But too often I try one and discover that I don't like what's inside. I love pieces filled with pecans or caramel, but when I bite into an orange crème, I have to force myself to finish it. I know there must be someone out there who simply loves the orange crème better than all the others. *I wish I had your address, I'd send you all mine. And by the way, you can have the raspberry gels, too.*

Just as we all like different flavors of chocolates, we are also different in our personality types, talents, passions, experiences, and spiritual gifts. Problems can develop in friendship if we don't give each other the freedom to be different.

If I try to make you act like me, we'll never be friends. If my friend is conventional and traditional and I am quirky and off-beat, our friendship can only be light, natural, and free if we accept each other for what and who we are.

GET OVER IT

My friend Anita Renfroe—author, singer, comedian, and Women of Faith speaker—is *free*. She loves life, finds the funny side in any situation, and thinks in Technicolor word pictures. She has learned to wear what she likes. Here's what she said recently to a group of Christian speakers about a woman's tendency to dress like everyone else.

> I am so incredibly over all the stage dressing rules where
> we all start to look like the Stepford speakers. It's so
> ungenuine and unexpressive of who we are individually.
> I would agree that we should be aware of modesty and
> camera issues, but beyond that, it should totally be what
> you look and feel great in and what most authentically
> expresses your personality. I think your clothes and hair
> and accessories should tip off the audience as to what to

expect from you before you ever open your mouth. Are you Miss Manners? Dress like it. Are you outrageous and loud? Dress like it. Don't let your personality and message be at odds with what you wear. Find a wardrobe trademark and make it yours. And a full-length mirror is your best friend. If we can ever get free of the Stepford thing, imagine what other areas could open up for us. Besides, I don't think any of us Davids can do well in Saul's armor. Be authentically you.[1]

Anita expresses the truth so well. Freedom starts with understanding who we are, what we do, and how we look. Then when we accept those traits and features, we can start to live free. We should try to get over ourselves and any tendencies we have to harshly judge ourselves.

> If you judge people, you have no time to love them.
> —MOTHER TERESA

I love the saying, "God don't make no junk." He made us exactly how He wants us to be. Don't put yourself down. Be the you God intended you to be.

A true friend allows you to be the individual that God made you to be. She also acknowledges that you may flounder. She will not reject you when you make mistakes and fail. Instead, she will encourage you to excel with no jealousy or rivalry. Freedom emancipates friendship from the slavery of pretense.

FRIENDSHIP ALLOWS FREEDOM

George and I have many preacher friends. It isn't because we are in the same profession; it's because of the freedom we give to each one when we spend time together. They are never expected to quote Scripture or give counseling advice. (Can you imagine the pressure that ministers feel most of the time?) Our friendship allows freedom.

I was eating in a restaurant one day when I overheard two girls behind me. One said, "I don't want to overstep any boundaries here." The other responded, "With friends there are no boundaries."

What freedom!

My friend Edith endures me when I'm me. I'm convinced that I could say the most awful thing and she wouldn't think badly of me. She doesn't judge me. She loves me enough to correct me and help me get back on the right path, but along the way she's willing to let me vent and sometimes rant.

Forrest Gump was right: life *is* like a box of chocolates. We're never sure what we are going to get when we bite into a day. In friendship, we need freedom to be authentic and genuine with each other. Sometimes that means accepting a trait or action in your friend that isn't her best. As friends, we urge each other to be better Christ followers, but we don't expect our friends to conform to unwritten behavior rules. We give freedom.

PEEL AWAY THE DISGUISES

Have you ever been to Glamour Shots? When you arrive, the makeup artist piles about a hundred pounds of makeup on your face, and your skin never looked so beautiful. The camera will pick up no flaw. Then she parts your hair down the middle of the back and pulls it all forward so that your photo will look like you have a lot of hair. Then she takes you into the studio and lets you put on dazzling clothes you don't have in your closet at home—fur and feathers and leather and gigantic earrings.

When I went for my session, the photos turned out just fabulous. I bought them all. I took them home to George, and he began to rave, "These are beautiful! What amazing photographs!" After a few minutes, he asked, "Who is it?"

On the other extreme, have you ever really looked at your driver's license photo? Not good. I think the technicians are trained to snap the picture at the worst time. Rarely are the photographs flattering.

Neither the glamorous shot nor the driver's license photo is a real representation of you. You probably aren't the mysterious woman in the Glamour Shot *(especially if your own husband can't recognize you),* and you certainly aren't that dowdy creature in your driver's license photo.

Unfortunately, we go through life wearing disguises and masks that keep the real person inside of us hidden. When I wrap my life up in disguises like chocolate covers up orange or raspberry crème, my pains, insecurities, doubts, and detachments are hidden away.

As women, we learn the mask technique early in life. What teenage girl hasn't begged her mother for the right shoes or jeans so she can fit in with the popular crowd? In an article in *O, The Oprah Magazine,* Melissa Bank expressed our collective longing for conformity as she remembered her teenage years: "My mother said, 'Just be yourself.' What I said to myself was, 'Just be like them.'"[2] We want to conform and not stand out in a negative way.

What makes us hide our pain and insecurities from each other? When we are lonely or doubting, why do we put on a mask and pretend all is well?

FREEDOM RESCUES

Chocolate-box freedom releases us from the binding chains of conformity. Friendship rescues us from the shackles of adjusting our lives to fit what we think everyone expects of us.

George and I teach the Bible to a group of single adults. These men and women carry heavy baggage from all that life has heaped on them. Some have lost a spouse to death. Others have experienced divorce. Many have prodigal children. All have learned to live with pain, loneliness, self-doubt, and financial stress. In the several years we have been with them, the group has grown into a family.

An interesting thing happens when a new person attempts to join our group. You see hesitation and uncertainty. You sense the walls the person has built for protection. But the group has been where the new person is. No matter what mess the person's life is in, the group is never shocked or offended. Soon acceptance and understanding encourage the newcomer to allow freedom in. Some have worn the disguise for years, but the group helps them unmask and experience true friendship.

FREE TO BE ME NO MATTER WHAT

When the producers were picking a friend for Lucy in the beginning days of the *I Love Lucy* show, the criteria were clear: "A best friend is someone who doesn't look at you as if you're crazy when you say something like, 'Let's steal John Wayne's cement footprints from in front of Grauman's Theatre.'"[3] Lucy and Ethel were great friends and an example of freedom. Whatever crazy stunt Lucy thought up, Ethel was there with support and loyalty. It was said of them,

> It's one of the blessings of old friends that you can afford to be stupid with them.
> —RALPH WALDO EMERSON

"Friends go the distance, friends make sacrifices, friends forgive, friends hold you up when you've had too much Vitameatavegamin."[4] Freedom doesn't stunt ideas—no matter how crazy they sound.

When Jonathan and David said good-bye to each other, knowing that one or both of them would not survive battle, they wept together. But the Bible says that "David wept the most."[5] Jonathan was the crown prince, yet he gave David liberty to weep. When your heart is broken, you can bleed all over an intimate friend and it will be okay.

Jesus relaxed when He was at Martha's house. Crowds pushed Him and chased Him all the time, like the paparazzi chase celebrities today. And He dealt with the slow-learning, slow-to-believe disciples. Every day was a challenge and a test. But when He went to Martha's and relaxed in a recliner with His shoes off, drinking one of Martha's famous cups of coffee and eating chocolate pie, He was free.

When you have an intimate friend, you shouldn't have to explain yourself. How open are you to your friend? Do you expect her to behave in a certain way? Or do you allow her to be herself, loving her anyway?

MY CHOCOLATE-TRUFFLE FRIEND

I smiled when I read the e-mail from Nancy Bauer, who has been my special friend since we first met years ago in a small group Bible study class. In her closing line, Nancy wrote, "To my chocolate-truffle friend, the best one in the box."

When Nancy and I first met, we connected immediately. We made time for each other in our hectic lives. Even when Nancy saw me at my worst, she never condemned me. From the beginning, she and I could talk about the deepest things in our hearts. I shared my frustration about how my frenzied schedule kept me from pursuing my dreams, and she shared her deepest concerns about family issues. We both loved the Bible and immersed ourselves in its truth and comfort. Our kids were about the same age, so we shared the joys and terrors of parenting.

Ours was a deep spiritual friendship. Nancy is everything I'm not but want to be. She is energetic yet calm, organized and creative. She is thoughtful and never misses encouraging those around her; she has a knack for sending cards on special occasions. She is genuinely concerned for the well-being of others.

Then I hired Nancy to work in my office, a busy, stressful, corporate headquarters for an international business. There she saw a side of me that never surfaced in our church or home environment. I am often forceful, scattered, and bossy. Instead of being thoughtful, I move like a freight train from one project to the next.

> As with most fine things, chocolate has its season. There is a simple memory aid that you can use to determine whether it is the correct time to order chocolate dishes: Any month whose name contains the letter *A*, *E*, or *U* is the proper time for chocolate.
> —SANDRA BOYNTON

Nancy now witnessed the side of me that I always tried to hide from her. Those pushy, domineering, self-important, superior, and mostly fussy features that surfaced in my position as the person in charge.

Yet Nancy stayed my friend, and in spite of my bad behavior, she loved me.

When Oprah Winfrey was asked to describe her friendship with Gayle King, she said that it's almost impossible to describe the bond they share. "How can you explain a level of intimacy where someone *always* loves you, *always* respects you, admires you?"[6]

Oprah is right. It is difficult to describe a chocolate-truffle friend. She's the one who hears you say something snide or profane but doesn't judge. She's a friend who watches your journey in life and doesn't expect perfection. She's the one who knows you didn't mean to hurt her feelings. She sees God working in your life, and she is willing to wait for the changes He is making. She knows mistakes are building blocks, so she doesn't flinch when you fail.

> Everything I eat should contain either garlic or chocolate, but rarely both.
> —AUTHOR UNKNOWN

Your chocolate-truffle friend revels in your mountaintops and identifies with your crashes. Nancy is my most enthusiastic cheerleader and encourager. As Oprah said, "Gayle is more excited about my success than I am. It makes her genuinely happy."[7]

As I thought about Nancy's friendship, I realized how remarkable it is that our bond is as strong as ever, even though we now live hundreds of miles apart. I asked her to put together a few paragraphs about our friendship from her perspective. Frankly, I was overwhelmed by what she wrote. As you read her words, I hope you will understand more clearly what "freedom" means in a friendship.

> When I met Karen, the ultimate Superwoman, she amazed me. She taught adult Sunday school, sang in the choir, sang beautiful solos, recited entire chapters of the Bible from memory, brought five covered dishes to every church function, cleaned the church kitchen afterward, served on committees, led overnight ladies' retreats, held an executive position with a large international firm, and frequently traveled on business, all in addition to being a devoted wife and mother of two.
>
> She never missed a church service or any event that involved her children, she routinely entertained large groups in her home, where she cooked everything from scratch, even the dessert—and served it on china. Where did she get all that energy? Later I learned that she survives on a limited amount of sleep. She's a morning person and has accomplished more by the time I get up in the morning than most of us do in eight hours.

Karen was surrounded by friends and loved by everyone. We bonded over our mutual love of God's Word and enjoyed a deep spiritual friendship; however, I had her so high on a pedestal that I thought she could do no wrong, so I was very protective of the image I had portrayed to her of myself, afraid that if she really got to know me, she would discover my faults and wouldn't want to be my friend.

Then I went to work in her office. I saw Karen, the executive. She was the boss. She was tough. She had to be tough to make it in a man's world, and I understood that. I was delighted to learn that she was human after all! As our masks came off and we moved from just friends to intimate sharing, our friendship blossomed into a level of freedom that is so liberating. We can be ourselves, just the way God made us, with no fear of judgment. What a remarkable gift that is.

Eleven years ago I moved away from Karen, but distance has not been a determent to our friendship. Whenever we get the chance to talk, it's like no time has passed. Our unmasked, free-to-be-ourselves friendship survives.

Five years after I moved away, life threw me
for a loop, and the first person I called was
Karen. When you are angry, hurting, and depressed,
you need a friend who loves the Lord, a friend
who will let you hurt, let you cry, not judge you
and love you in spite of your faults and failures.
That's the kind of friend I have in Karen; when
I called her that day, she listened, she loved me,
and she prayed for me over the phone. Her words
were a healing balm. She is a gift from God and
I treasure her above all friends; she truly is the
chocolate truffle, the best one in the box!

The most amazing thing about the evolution of my friendship with Nancy is that we both started out trying to hide our bad features. I wanted her to think of me as Superwoman and Super Christian. She wanted me to see her as Bible Student and Godly Woman. Working in the same office forced us to remove our masks; as a result, our friendship not only deepened but also realized new freedom. Every friendship deserves to know the freedom that comes from removing masks.

An intimate friend doesn't preach a sermon. Instead, she lets you hurt. Lets you cry. Lets you be yourself and experiences your hurt alongside you.

Bringing the Chocolate

1. Make a list of three traits that make you unique. Do you hide any of those traits because you think your friends won't understand? How do you disguise yourself to conform to your friends' expectations?

2. Would you describe your mask as being more like a Glamour Shot or a driver's license photo? If a friend offered you total freedom, what might your snapshot look like then?

3. What liberty do you offer your friends?

4. Who is your chocolate-truffle friend? Write her a letter and express why you think she is the best one in the box.

Prayer
Dear Lord, make me a freedom place.
Help me lavishly offer freedom to my friend.

Offering Chocolate to My Friend
Dear friend, I offer you freedom. You can be open, honest, and real with me. I promise not to judge you.

The Best One in the Box
Ingredients:
2 cups semisweet chocolate chips

4 ounces unsweetened chocolate

1 14-oz. can sweetened condensed milk

Topping Options:

Powdered sugar

Cocoa powder

Toasted coconut

Finely chopped toasted nuts

Candy sprinkles

Directions:

Melt chocolate in microwave, stirring every thirty seconds. When chocolate is completely melted, add sweetened condensed milk and stir until smooth.

Place mixture in refrigerator and cool until firm enough to roll into balls. Using a melon baller or a rounded tablespoon, scoop and roll mixture into two-inch balls. Roll each truffle in the topping of your choice. Transfer to a parchment-lined baking sheet, then cover and chill for at least one hour.

Hot Chocolate Around the Home Fire

Keep on loving each other as brothers. Do not forget
to entertain strangers, for by so doing some people
have entertained angels without knowing it.

HEBREWS 13:1–2

Put a smile on your face, make the world a better place.
HERSHEY'S CHOCOLATE SLOGAN

When I was a year old, my six-year-old brother, Jimmy, knocked on every door around the neighborhood to invite people to my birthday party. Imagine my mother's surprise when the guests began to arrive. No party was planned. She grabbed snacks from the pantry while Daddy rushed to the grocery store for ice cream. In the end, the "nonparty" was a big success because my parents' home was always open to friends and strangers.

It doesn't matter how much faith, encouragement, forgiveness, loyalty, joy, freedom, or chocolate we give; unless we open our doors, we don't have real friendship. Inviting a friend into your home is the perfect topping for friendship, just like real whipped cream on a cup of hot chocolate.

In his book *Virtual America*, George Barna reported the results of his research about friendship. He found that most Americans are finding it harder and harder to make meaningful, lasting friends. Fifty-five percent of non-Christians feel it is hard to make friends, and 73 percent of evangelical Christians consider forming friendships difficult.[1] These numbers are shocking because Christ followers should have common ground to build on and a deep desire for significant friendships.

> Nobody knows
> the truffles I've seen!
> —GEORGE LANG

According to Robert Putnam in *Bowling Alone*, America is experiencing an epidemic of loneliness. Putnam explains that pressures like time and money, cities that sprawl across several counties, and obsession with TV prevent people from participating in organizations. Memberships dwindle every year in bridge clubs, veterans' groups, charity guilds, alumni organizations, Elks and other lodges, churches, garden clubs, PTAs, and bowling leagues. These groups' numbers are no longer being replenished by the next generation. People don't join organizations as often and as a result become isolated and lonely. The negative effect on our society is dramatic.[2]

WHATEVER HAPPENED TO HOSPITALITY?

The early Christians met in different people's homes and shared meals. In my grandparents' time, if someone dropped by, they often stayed the night. My mother always cooked a roast for Sunday dinner, and my parents frequently invited people over for a meal after church. Our generation invites people over only occasionally, and my children's generation goes out to eat. The phrase "come on over to our house" is no longer in our lexicon.

Spending time together in people's homes is one of the basic building blocks of friendship. Am I willing to invest time in my friends—to plan and prepare so that we can enjoy each other's company?

Perhaps the main reason we aren't more hospitable is that we're concerned about how our house looks. But a true friend is less focused on making her house perfect than she is on loving her friends.

PEOPLE NEED PEOPLE

Though it becomes less and less easy in the twenty-first century to make friends, it is nevertheless important. We were created with a need for others. Time with other people stimulates us intellectually and spiritually. There are even health benefits associated with friendship—research has shown that maintaining

Ill Bring the Chocolate

strong friendships is as beneficial to one's physical well-being as quitting smoking.

Friendships are solidified when we bring others into our home. Almost daily, I receive one or more e-mails that contain a cute poem or story about friendship. Nearly every e-mail contains a stanza or paragraph about inviting friends to your home, like this: "True hospitality speaks for itself. Hospitality is the language of the heart of God. A Jewish rabbi noted that hospitality, in the fullest meaning of that word, is as close as we will ever get to the face of God."[3]

As Christians, we are called on by God to break the cycle of isolation and loneliness. The Bible says, "Don't copy the behavior and customs of this world, but be a new and different person with a fresh newness in all you do and think."[4] Christ loved people and formed deep, rich friendships with His disciples and with friends like Mary, Martha, and Lazarus. He visited the homes of Simon and Zacchaeus and Peter. Paul instructed us to "love each other with brotherly affection and take delight in honoring each other."[5]

Pastor Andy Stanley believes that the most important thing he does in ministry is his Monday night meeting. Even though he preaches to more than 16,000 people on Sunday, every Monday Andy and his wife open their home to a small group of six to eight people. Then every twelve to eighteen months, those six to eight people go out to form new groups, and six to eight new people begin meeting in the Stanleys' home. In this way, Pastor Stanley makes friends and keeps his finger on the pulse of the real issues facing people.[6] No one can deny that a huge part of the church's success is because this couple opens their home in hospitality.

THE HOSPITALITY HABIT

The Bible commands us to make hospitality a habit in our home: "Get into the habit of inviting guests home for dinner."[7] That means doing it over and over again until it feels natural.

When we lived in The Woodlands, our church started growing so fast that we found ourselves not knowing the people worshiping in the same row. George and I decided we wanted to get to know as many people as we could, so every Saturday we looked in the church directory, called people we hadn't met, and invited them to lunch on Sunday. The replies were sometimes comical. Some were hesitant, but most came. We love to cook, so we set a big, long table and passed bowls of mostly plain home cooking around to strangers. Before long, the table was filled with great conversation and laughter.

One woman asked us, "Why do you do this?"

Our answer was easy. "It's a new tradition, a habit; it feels natural."

When was the last time someone other than your family put

their feet under your table? You can start a new habit by inviting friends over to share a meal. The Bible says, "Cheerfully share your home with those who need a meal or a place to stay for the night."[8] If you share a meal, friendship will follow. Those people who started out as strangers became more than mere acquaintances. They are now friends because we shared a meal around our table.

As Pastor Rick Warren said, "People are not looking for a friendly church; they are looking for friends."

IT'S THE WAY JESUS WOULD LIVE IN THIS CENTURY

Our son, Brett, describes how friendship is the key to building the kingdom of God:

> I realized that I've tried to make sharing Christ all about a planned event or a system (almost a hidden agenda). It seems like in Acts, the focus was on BEING a follower of Jesus and not really about planning a way to tell people about him. If we just "be" a follower, then Colossians 3:17 really can come to life of "whatever [we] do, whether in word or deed, do it all in the name of the Lord Jesus." This seems to give so much freedom to live life simply in the name of Jesus. No major plans, no major schemes. In Acts, the first church followed the example of Jesus by being a part of the community (hanging out with people)

and whatever they were doing. No plan except living the name of Jesus in your world. Seems freeing and simple.[9]

Our day-to-day living is the most important and effective way to reach, serve, and befriend others. We don't need a plan; we need a purpose. Otherwise we may find ourselves just living and not really reaching. Life gets so busy with "stuff," time passes so quickly, and before we know it, we have gone weeks, months, even years without specifically being a friend.

I once heard a speaker ask, "Do you plan to be alive for the next nine years? How many people will you impact? What is your plan to do it?" We don't need a specific method or program; we just need to reach out to others. We do that by opening our home.

> Forget love—
> I'd rather fall in chocolate!
> —AUTHOR UNKNOWN

George and I live in a community, but we can't just live there. Instead we must focus on ways to interact with people—get to know them and let them get to know us. When they see our open doors and open hearts, opportunities for friendship and spiritual interaction will happen. But if I don't open my doors, if I continue to live my secluded life in the woods, I won't ever make friends. None of my neighbors are going to knock on the door and ask, "Will you be my friend? Can you show me how to become a follower of Jesus?"

BUT I DON'T KNOW HOW

Your gift of hospitality may revolve around your love of cooking or your easygoing personality. Perhaps you are an engaging story-teller with the ability to charm and fascinate people for hours. No matter what your gift, you have a lot to offer. So if you can't cook well, don't fret. If you love them, it won't matter what you serve. As Pastor John Ortberg once said, "Better to eat Twinkies with friends than broccoli alone."

You can set a nice table even if you don't own matching glasses or delicate china. Over the years I've collected inexpensive clear glass salad plates and bowls to complement the interesting dinner plates I pick up at sales and warehouse stores. I can dramatically change the look of my table by using the colorful dinner plates, even though I use the same clear accessories each time.

> My therapist told me the best way to attain happiness is to finish what I've started. So far, I've finished half a bag of chocolate-chip cookies and a chocolate cake.
> I feel better already.
> —DAVE BARRY

If you don't own china or pottery, go with paper or plastic. Stores are filled with plenty of durable, disposable wares that are beautiful. Look through magazines and books for ideas, then assemble these photos in a three-ring binder. Add fun napkins folded in interesting shapes, or roll them up and tie with matching ribbons. Personalized place cards solve the problem of who sits where, and they also say, "I think you are special, and I want you to be here."

Play appropriate music softly in the background. Greet your guests personally and warmly when they arrive. Serve a platter of finger foods alongside tall glasses of tea or lemonade to ease any awkward beginnings. For the meal, cook something you've successfully cooked before and plate it in an interesting, colorful way. Even simple food looks beautiful on a plate when enhanced with dark green parsley, curly lettuce, or a bright red tomato. If you don't cook, buy the food and serve it on your plates. Remember, the food is much less important than the friendship.

OBSTACLES TO HOSPITALITY

It seems everyone I know is short on time. I'm sure you are wondering how to find this kind of time for friends.

Fortunately, we have communication technology that helps us stay in touch: personal day planners, e-mail, cell phones, and quick mail service. These tools help us plan our schedules so that we can make time for friends. Careful planning and a determined choice to become a hospitable friend will help you overcome the obstacles of time management.

If you set your mind to being a hospitable friend, opportunities will show up in unusual moments. One group I know gets together once a week on Sunday evenings. They invite friends and make tuna sandwiches. They call the event simply "tuna." It's a casual comfortable evening for friends and family to be together.

This, to me, is the definition of hospitality: easy, gentle, uncomplicated.

HOSPITALITY WITH A PURPOSE

Hospitality is more than entertaining. Its purpose is developing or strengthening friendship and sharing the love of Christ. You are sharing Jesus when you share yourself. Loving people is a Christ follower's specialty because Jesus loved people.

When your guests arrive, ask them about themselves. People who are urged to talk about themselves will think *you* are a good conversationalist. Inquire about the details of their lives. Care about their situation.

My daughter, Cherry, likes to find out some trivial fact about each of her guests beforehand. Then she makes up little cards that read "Who at this table _____?" It's a great icebreaker and keeps the conversation flowing throughout the evening.

When George and I threw those Sunday dinners for guests, we always reserved two chairs for Steve and Joni, our pastor and his wife. The lunch was a great opportunity for the two of them to get to know new people in our rapidly growing church. Joni always found a moment during the meal to ask someone at the table to talk about when he or she became a Christ follower. The conversation would shift to spiritual matters, and those deep, warm-as-hot-chocolate friendships would begin to form.

We love football in Texas, and in my family we especially love Texas Aggie football. We read everything printed and online about the team and the season. In an article by Mark Beech, a story about the team bonding in friendship caught my eye: "The spark for Texas A&M's surprising season was struck last December, after a bitterly disappointing 5-6 campaign. That's when…a handful of [teammates] began talking about how to revive a team they felt was lacking cohesion. The group came up with an idea: house parties, albeit without kegs and coeds. Building Champions is what the players dubbed the bonding sessions, held every week in the home of one teammate from January through July. Just a bunch of guys getting together."[10]

Gatherings in your home will build friendships and develop deep bonds like no other activity. Or, as one Aggie quarterback said about the newfound team friendships, "We play for each other."

Soup's On

Writer Julie Dahlberg wrote about how her husband, Scott, and their three children—all under seven—officially started a weekly Soup Night for their neighborhood. Because they were responsible only for making soup, there were no grand menus to plan. So

Julie and her kids hand-delivered invitations to their neighbors that read, "Come one Thursday, come any Thursday. Bring a loaf of bread, salad, dessert, or nothing but a smile. No RSVP necessary."

Julie was nervous just before the initial dinner, but as soon as the first guest walked through the door, her worries melted away. "The conversation was easy, and the soup, to my delight, was a big hit."[11] Friendships developed because Julie and her family opened the door of their home with a welcoming invitation.

FRIENDSHIP HOSPITALITY PLANS

In her book *Girlfriend Gatherings,* Janet Holm McHenry writes about how she and a group of high-school buddies made time to renew and revitalize their longtime friendships:

> And so I answered Linda's e-mail: "Yes, let's get together." And about a month later nine of the twelve friends we were able to reach joined us in our first Girlfriend Brunch, which we have since decided will become a five-year tradition. And yes, others were grieving the loss of parents. And several were walking through the slough of divorce. But we instantly connected that morning of our thirtieth reunion. And we decided that reconnecting gave us such joy and a sense of importance of our past that we would not wait for another five years to pass. We would keep in touch with a round robin letter.[12]

Set aside a weekend to get together with some of your oldest friends. Plan a weekend retreat. Go to someone's lake house or country cabin. Spend some time fellowshiping for the sole purpose of building those friendships.

MENU PANIC

Preparing food for your guests should not become a panic situation. To choose a menu, think first about how the food will look on the plate. Plan a meat, a starch, and a vegetable. For example, chicken, rice, and green beans; or steak, potato, and salad.

Consider your combination of colors. (Everything shouldn't be beige.) Choose colorful vegetables such as tomatoes, carrots, or corn, and leafy green vegetables to add contrast and make the plate visually appealing.

Consider also your combination of flavors. As a general rule, don't mix ethnic dishes, like Italian pasta with Mexican beans.

> The problem: How to get two pounds of chocolate home from the store in a hot car. The solution: Eat it in the parking lot.
> —AUTHOR UNKNOWN

Once you've decided on a menu, practice making the meal several times. Cherry has a favorite menu combination of grilled chicken, grilled pineapple, green-bean bundles, and twice-baked potatoes. She marinates boneless chicken breasts in bottled marinade and slices thick rounds of fresh pineapple for the grill. A few days before the party, she gathers handfuls of green beans into bundles and wraps them in cooked bacon slices. After arranging the bundles in a baking dish, she pours a mixture of brown sugar, soy sauce, and garlic salt over them. On another day before the party, she bakes her potatoes in the oven. After baking, she cuts the potatoes in half, scoops out the middle (keeping the shells intact), and then mixes the potato flesh with sour cream, butter, chives, and tiny shrimp. Finally, she scoops the mixture back into the half-potato shells and covers each with cheese. On the day of the party, she grills the chicken and pineapple, bakes the beans and potatoes, and is free to enjoy her guests.

This is Cherry's trademark meal. She cooks it with the same ease for intimate groups of four as for sit-down dinners of 150. The food looks like it came from a gourmet restaurant, but she is not tired or flustered for the party.

You can develop your own trademark meal too. If you practice it over and over, it will be a huge success and you will love serving it.

Bringing the Chocolate

1. Make a list of friends and acquaintances who have never been to your home. Pick two or three, then call each one. Invite her over for hot chocolate.
2. Sit quietly for thirty minutes and think about what really keeps you from inviting friends to your home. What can you do to overcome that obstacle?

3. Read the story of Martha and Mary in Luke 10:38–42. Which character in the story do you most resemble? Who do you most admire? Assuming the one you resemble and the one you most admire aren't the same, how can you become more like the latter?

4. In the space below, write out a simple menu for lunch or dinner. Now invite someone over to enjoy it together.

_____

_____

_____

_____

Prayer
Dear Lord, build in me a heart for hospitality.

Offering Chocolate to My Friend
Dear friend, come on over to my house.
You are always welcome.

Fireside Hot Chocolate
Ingredients:

2 1-oz. squares of unsweetened chocolate, finely chopped

1 14-oz. can sweetened condensed milk

4 cups boiling water

1 teaspoon pure vanilla extract

Whipped cream, chocolate syrup (optional, to garnish)

Directions:

Melt the unsweetened chocolate in a large microwave-safe bowl, stirring every thirty seconds. Whisk in the sweetened condensed milk, then the vanilla, and finally the four cups of boiling water. Stir until smooth.

Pour into large mugs and, if desired, top with whipped cream and chocolate syrup.

Afterword

I worked in the U.S. grain industry for more than thirty years. My job was demanding, stressful, and highly charged, with multimillion-dollar deals relying upon quick, accurate decisions. Being the first woman to tackle this male-dominated industry complicated the job and compelled me to work long, focused hours.

In the process of trading rice to more than fifty countries, I swapped the need for friendship with the allure of accomplishment. I deliberately set out to be the hard businesswoman, and I didn't mind stepping on others to climb the ladder of success.

After a long while, I discovered that no success, job title, "deal," or company is an adequate substitute for the beauty and flavor of friendship. It was too late to save some of my friendships, but I made up my mind to seek out, acquire, and treasure friends from then on. The things I learned from those experiences are what you read in this book.

I pray that you will now begin your own quest to fill your life with chocolate-covered friends who love you, cherish you, help you, forgive you, laugh with you, and upon whom you will reciprocate by showering encouragement, lending faith, offering freedom, and opening your doors.

Let chocolate be your cue to be a friend.

Notes

Introduction

1. Don Miller, "The President's Corner," *Houston Business Journal*, August 27, 1984, 6a.

2. Mitsugi Saotome, www.wisdomquotes.com/002606.html

3. Linda Wallace, used with permission.

4. Cindy McMinimam, used with permission.

Chapter 1

1. Elaine Sherman, *Madame Chocolate's Book of Divine Indulgences* (Columbus, OH: McGraw-Hill/Contemporary, 1987), 12.

2. Romans 14:17, NLT.

3. There are also "failure to thrive" studies where orphaned babies who weren't held or cuddled actually died from lack of attention.

4. Hebrews 10:24, NASB.

5. Psalm 34:18.

6. Inspired by paragraphs from Vickie Kraft, *The Influential Woman*, (Dallas, TX: Word, 1992), 16.

7. 1 Thessalonians 5:11, MSG.

8. Janet Kornblum, "Meet My 5,000 New Best Pals," *USA Today*, September 10, 2006, D1.

9. 1 Thessalonians 2:8.

Chapter 2

1. Rick Warren, *The Purpose Driven Life* (Grand Rapids, MI: Zondervan, 2002), 142.
2. Matthew 8:5–10.
3. Hebrews 10:32–33, 35.
4. 2 Corinthians 4:18.
5. Author's notes.
6. Matthew 8:27.
7. Matthew 14:33.
8. Hebrews 11:3.
9. Taken from "Where the Action Is," a sermon by Rev. S. M. Lockridge; used with permission.
10. Romans 5:8.
11. John 5:24.
12. These three layers of faith are described in the first five verses of Hebrews 11. In verse 3, God created all things and without Him nothing was made. In verse 4, Abel brought a blood sacrifice typifying the eventual blood offering that Christ would make on the cross. In verse 5, Enoch walked with God and so can we.
13. Isaiah 61:1.
14. Hebrews 11:6.
15. Job 6:14.
16. Jeremiah 32:17.
17. Acts 27:33–36.

18. T. W. Hunt, "The Mind of Christ" video series, LifeWay
    Publishers.

Chapter 3

1. As quoted by Raymond McHenry, *In Other Words* (Houston,
    TX: Raymond McHenry Publisher, 1996), 82.
2. Hebrews 6:18–19.
3. 1 Samuel 23:15–16.
4. Martha Beck, "The Relationship Two-Step," *O, The Oprah
    Magazine*, August 2006, 47.
5. Acts 15:31.
6. Acts 15:32.
7. 2 Corinthians 5:18, NCV.
8. Mark 4:39, KJV.
9. Matthew 8:8.
10. Author's paraphrase of 2 Corinthians 5:20.
11. Hebrews 3:12–13.
12. Romans 1:11–12.
13. Romans 1:12, MSG.

Chapter 4

1. 1 John 3:18–19, MSG.
2. Proverbs 27:9, MSG.
3. Romans 14:17.
4. Romans 14:19.

5. Meditation 17, from *Devotions Upon Emergent Occasions* (1624), as quoted in *Norton Anthology of English Literature*, fifth edition (New York: W. W. Norton, 1962), vol. 1, 1107.

6. Matthew 19:27; Mark 10:28; see Luke 18:28.

7. John 15:15, MSG.

8. Philippians 2:1–8.

9. Bob Minzesheimer, "Friendship Eases Pain of Loss for 9/11 Widows," *USA Today*, September 5, 2006, 1a–2a.

10. Minzesheimer, "Friendship Eases Pain."

Chapter 5

1. Karen Porter, *Intimate Encounters with God* (Colorado Springs, CO: Cook Communications, 2003), 124.

2. 1 Peter 3:9.

3. Psalm 65:3.

4. Psalm 78:38–39.

5. Matthew 18:21–22.

6. Matthew 18:23–35.

7. 2 Corinthians 2:7–8.

8. Colossians 3:13–14.

9. Kari West and Noelle Quinn, *When He Leaves* (Colorado Springs, CO: Chariot Victor, 1998), 152.

10. Hebrews 10:24, NASB.

11. I have these five words written in the front flap of my Bible; I wish I knew where I first heard or read them so I could give credit.

12. Denise George, "What Forgiveness Isn't," *Today's Christian Woman*, July 2006, 39.

13. Matthew 5:23–24, MSG.

14. Judy Hampton, *Under the Circumstances* (Colorado Springs, CO: NavPress, 2001), 55.

Chapter 6

1. 2 Corinthians 7:3–4.

2. Margo Jefferson, "The Best Review I Ever Got," *O, The Oprah Magazine*, August 2006, 194.

3. C. S. Lewis, *Surprised by Joy* (London: Harper Collins, 1955), 93.

4. Jefferson, "The Best Review I Ever Got."

5. Valerie Monroe, "Friends Don't Let Friends," *O, The Oprah Magazine*, August 2006, 208.

6. 2 Corinthians 7:5.

7. 2 Corinthians 7:6–7.

8. Psalm 18:16.

9. Proverbs 27:10, TLB.

Chapter 7

1. Isaiah 65:19.

2. Luke 2:10.

3. Matthew 2:10.

4. Matthew 5:11–12, MSG.

5. See Acts 13:52.

6. Joyce Landorf, *Mourning Song* (Georgetown, TX: Balcony, 1995), 24.

7. See Luke 1:14, 44.

8. Romans 12:15, MSG.

9. John Ortberg, "He could have just said, 'And now, ladies, praise…'" as quoted in *Help, I Can't Stop Laughing* by Ann Spangler (Grand Rapids, MI: Zondervan, 2006), 79.

10. 1 Timothy 4:4, MSG.

11. Philippians 4:1, MSG.

Chapter 8

1. Anita Renfroe, used with permission. Read more about Anita at www.anitarenfroe.com.

2. Melissa Bank, "I Can't Believe I Said That," *O, The Oprah Magazine*, August 2006, 191.

3. Madelyn Pugh Davis, "Lucy and Ethel, Behind the Scenes," *O, The Oprah Magazine*, August 2006, 196.

4. Dan Shaw, "Everything I Needed to Know About Friendship I Learned from *I Love Lucy*," *O, The Oprah Magazine*, August 2006, 196.

5. 1 Samuel 20:41.

6. Lisa Kogan, "Oprah and Gayle Uncensored," *O, The Oprah Magazine*, August 2006, 188.

7. Kogan, "Oprah and Gayle."

Chapter 9

1. George Barna, *Virtual America: What Every Church Leader Needs to Know About Ministering in an Age of Spiritual and Technological Revolution* (Ventura, CA: Regal Books, 1993).

2. Robert D. Putnam, *Bowling Alone: The Collapse and Revival of American Community* (New York: Simon and Schuster, 2001).

3. Chuck and Kathie Crismier, *The Power of Hospitality* (Richmond, VA: Elijah Books, 2005), 23.

4. Romans 12:2, TLB.

5. Romans 12:10, TLB.

6. Andy Stanley, video on leadership, used with permission.

7. Romans 12:13, TLB.

8. 1 Peter 4:9, TLB.

9. Brett Porter, pastor of The Sanctuary in Mississagua, Ontario, Canada; used with permission. Read more about The Sanctuary at www.thesanctuary.ca and www.xanga.com/brettand kathryn.

10. Mark Beech, "Inside College Football: Arm in Arm," SI.com, November 2006.

11. Julie Dahlberg, "Soup's On, How One Family Serves up Neighborly Friendship," *Today's Christian Woman,* September/October 2004, 64.

12. Janet Holm McHenry, *Girlfriend Gatherings* (Eugene, OR: Harvest House, 2001), 16.